Dedicated to Isla Rose

Published in 2016
Artbat publishing.uk
email: art-trail-sw9@hotmail.co.uk

ISBN: 978-0-9935730-2-6

# Creative Journey Through Art
## Book Two
## Adults Only Colouring Book

(This book contains adult material)
(Not suitable for young children)

As a child growing up in Lancashire I would draw faces in the margins of my schoolbooks and dreamt of becoming an artist. I have continued in the arts and crafts ever since.

A small part of my 'fine art' practice, these drawings seem to take on a life of their own. I am fascinated by the way they appear when I put pen to paper and am happy to share these drawings with you in the hope you have as much fun as I have taking them further into colour.

This book includes some images from the series of drawings 'Speak To Me Softly' and two drawings from Creative Journey Through Art - Book One. There are also some cropped drawings, vignettes, for you to finish using your own skill and imagination.

Use an A5 paper mount or frame to showcase your finished work.

Margaret Lynn x

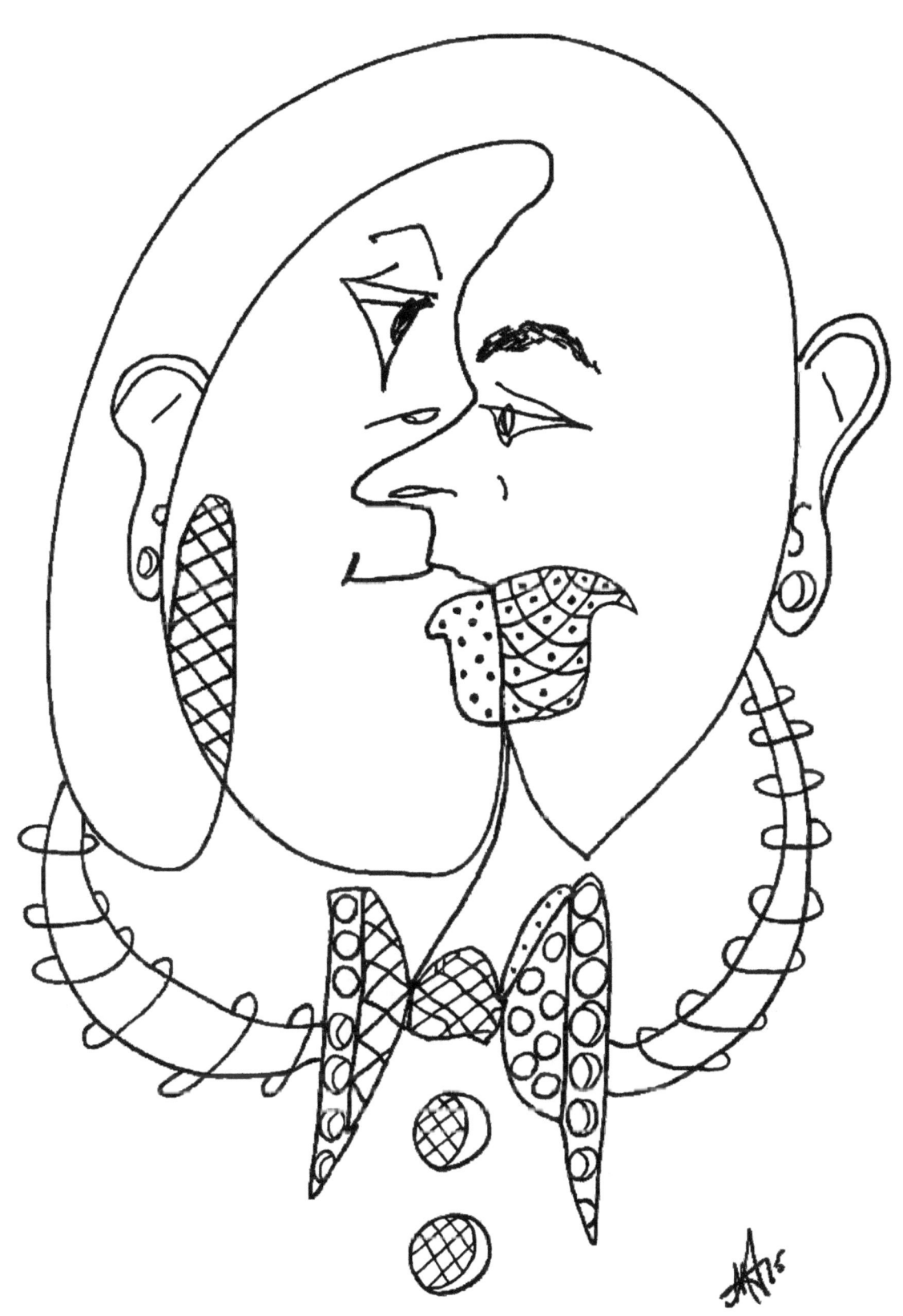

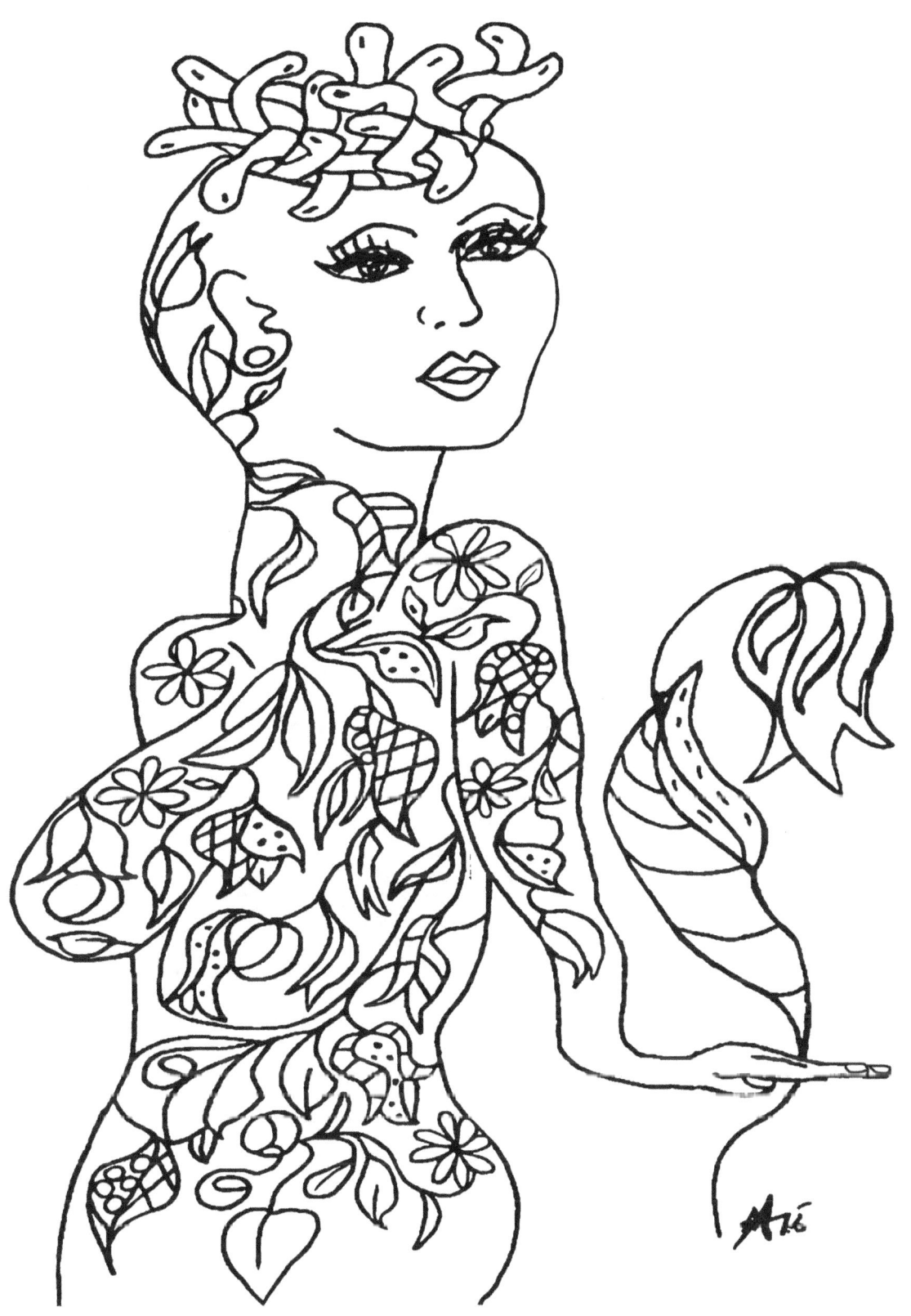

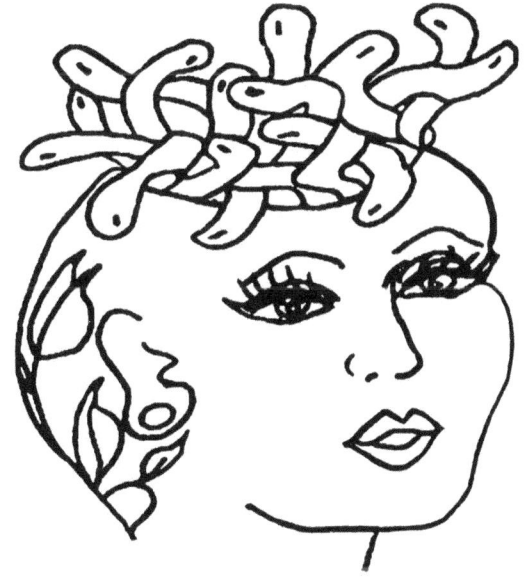

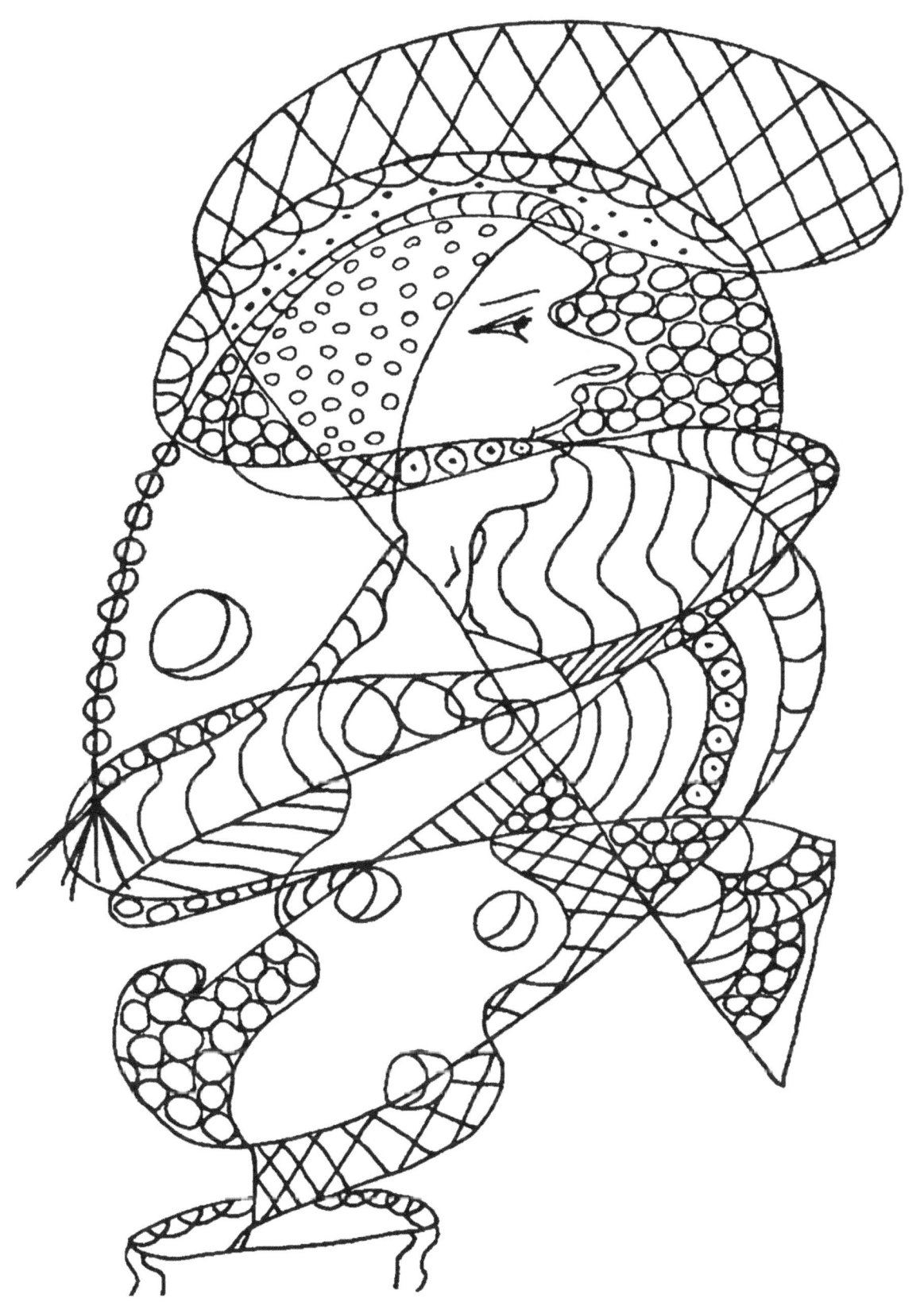

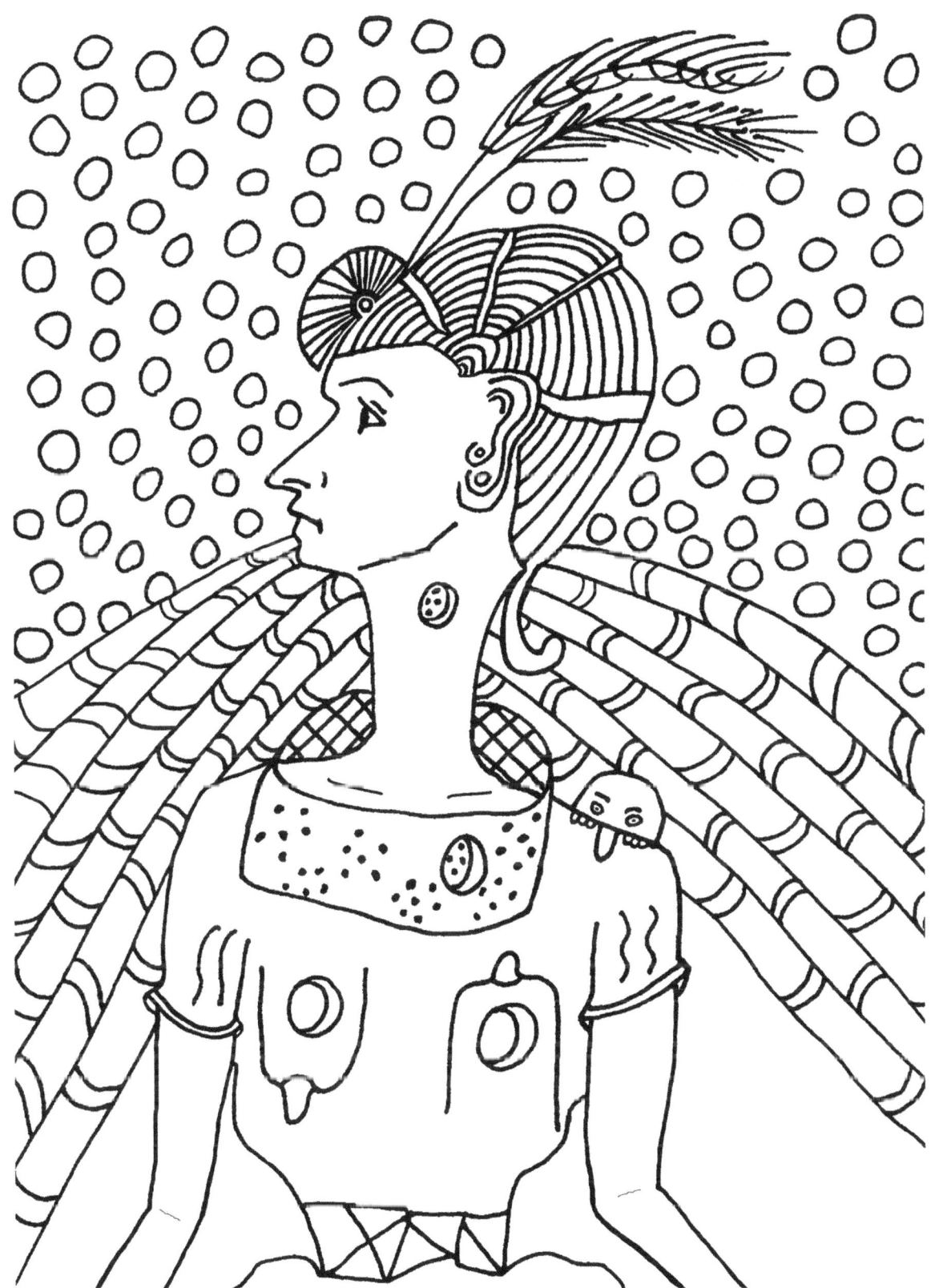

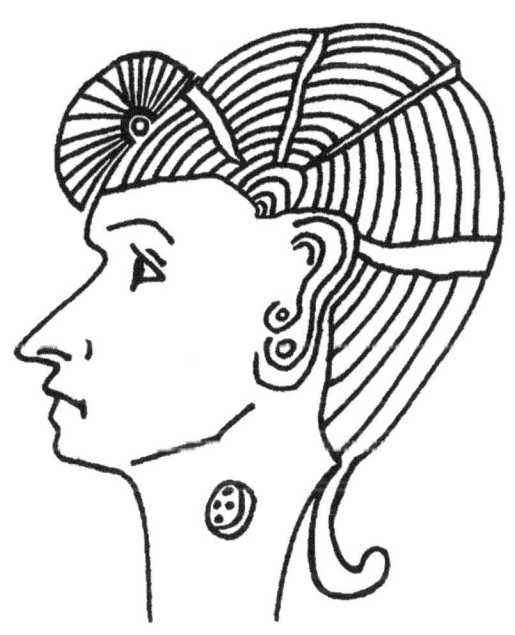

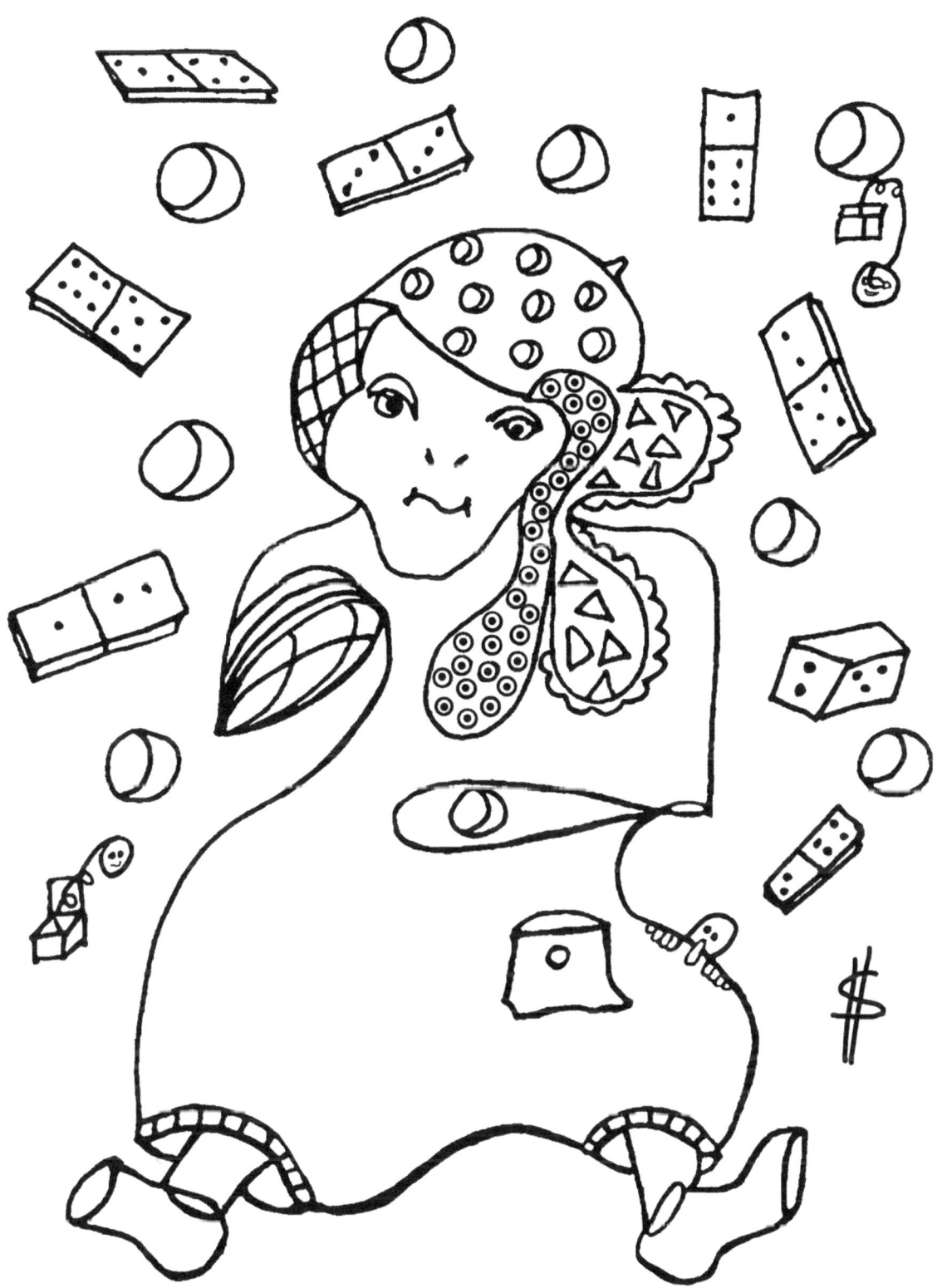

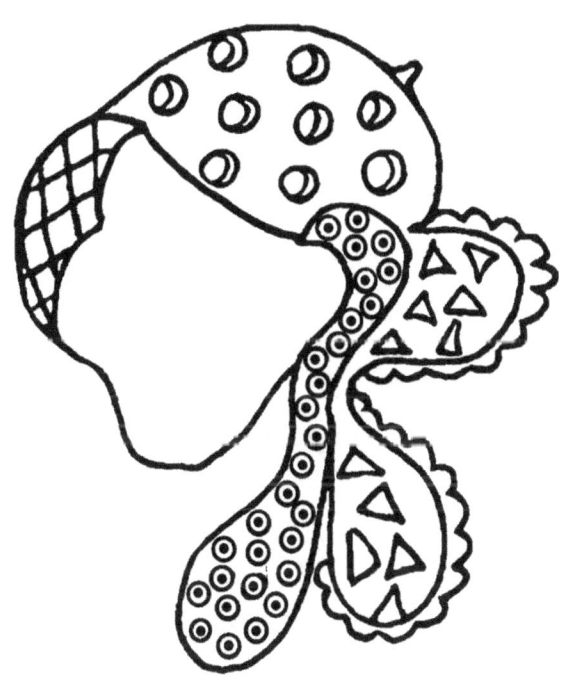

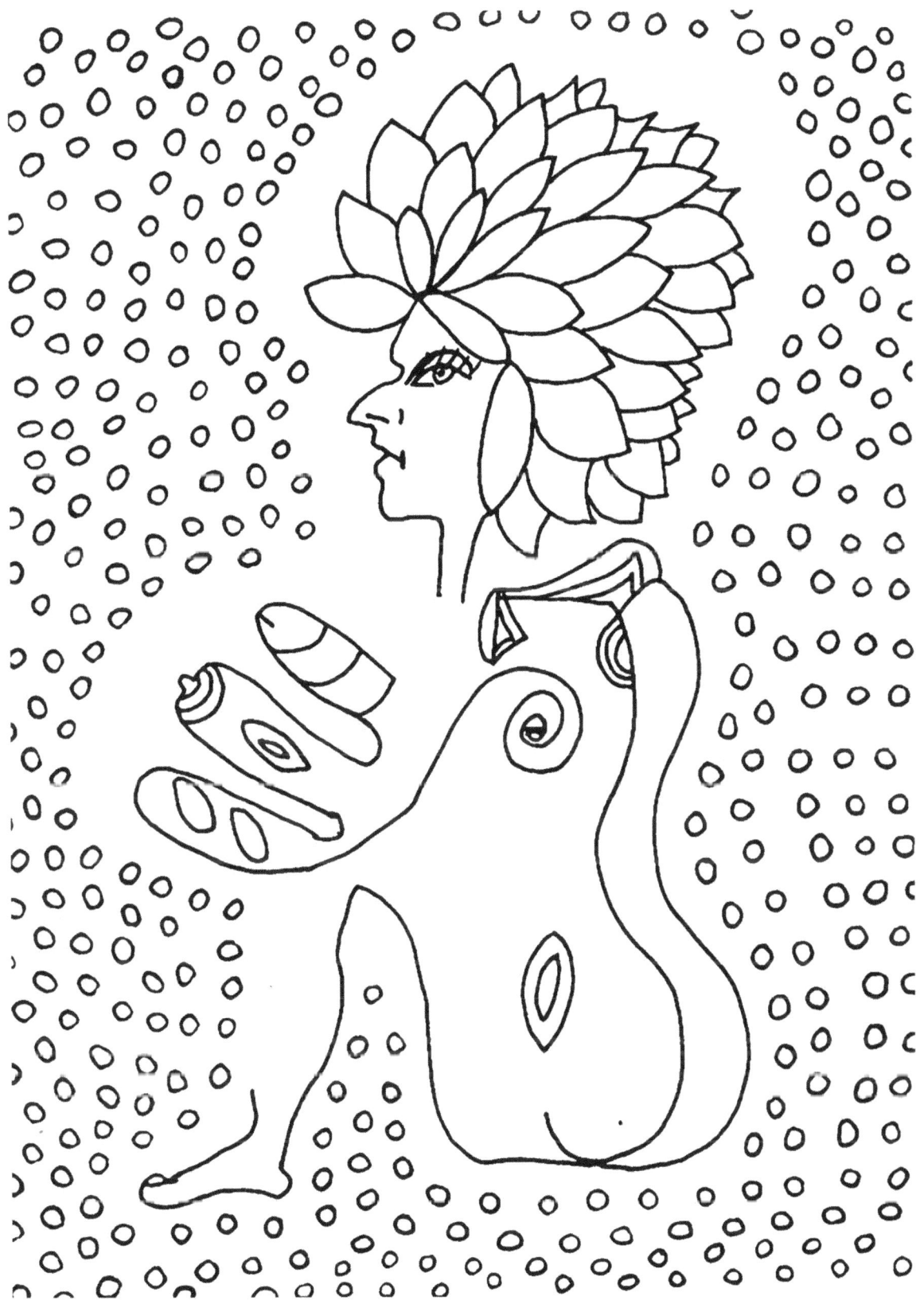

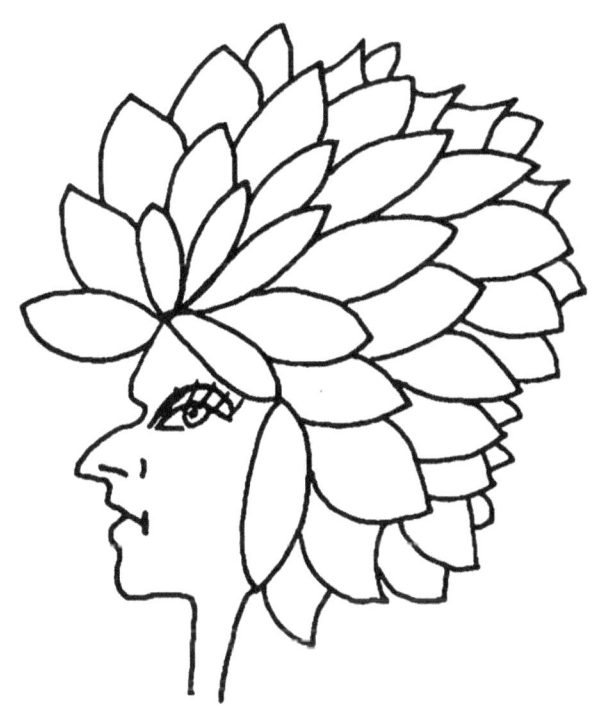

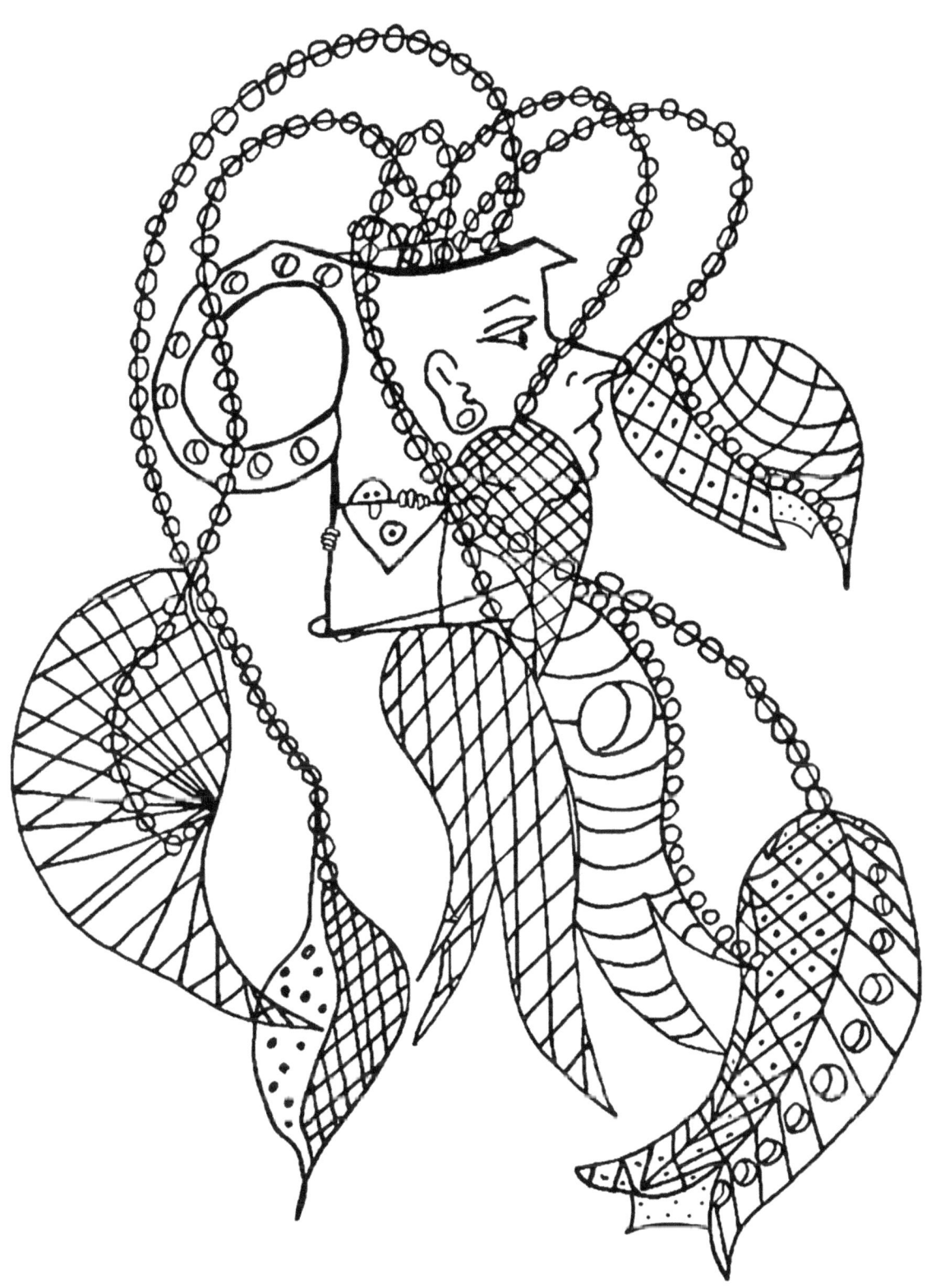

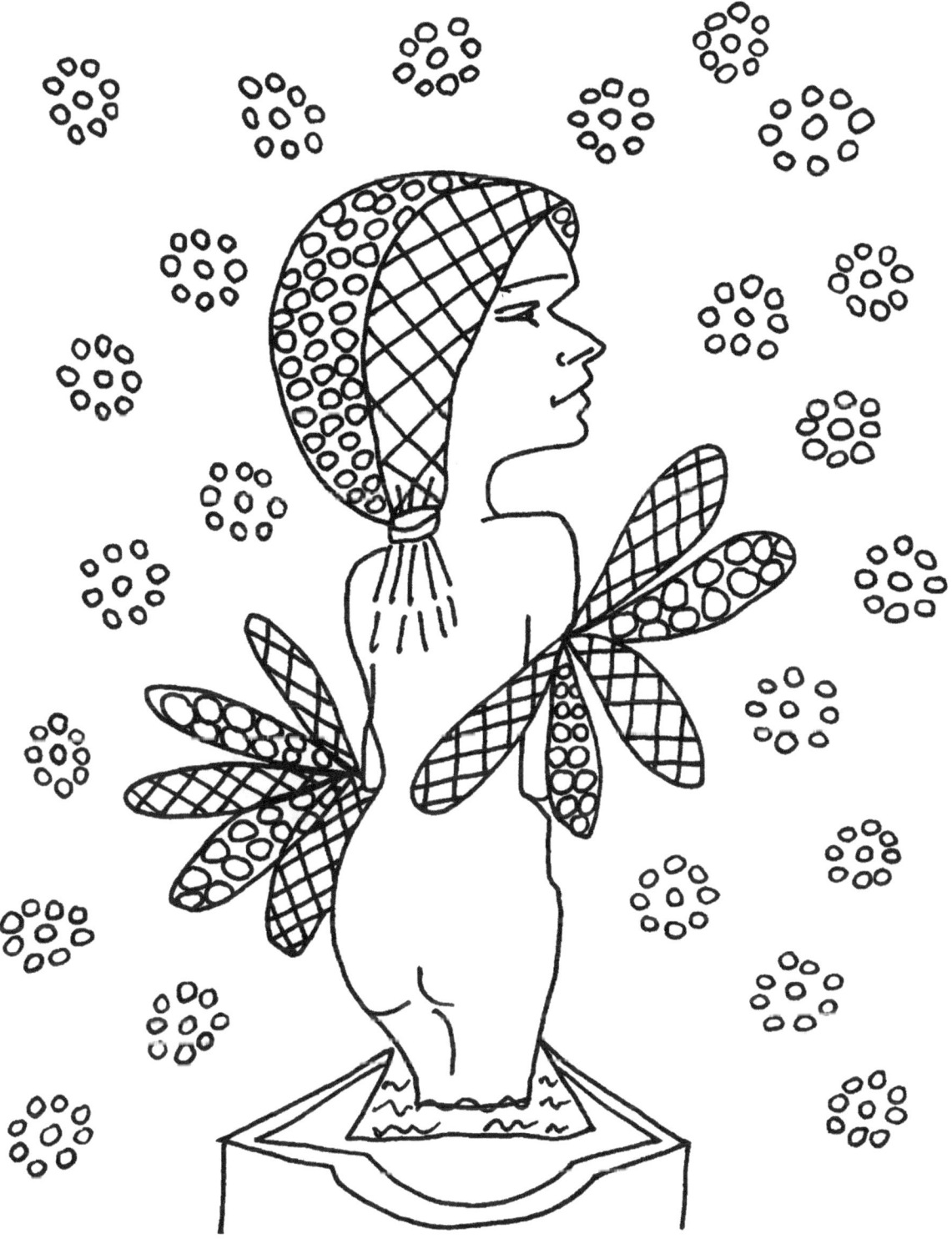

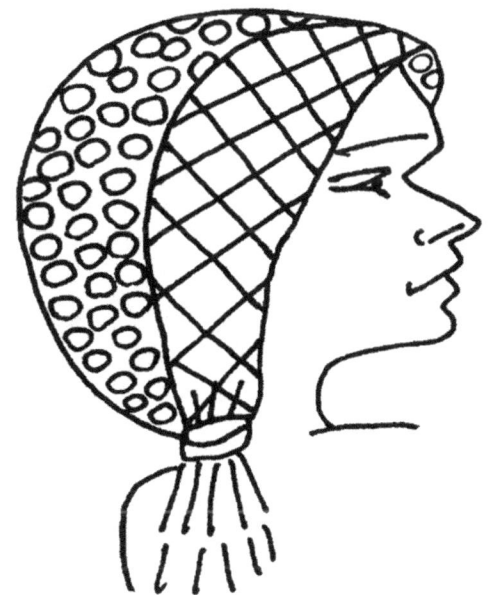

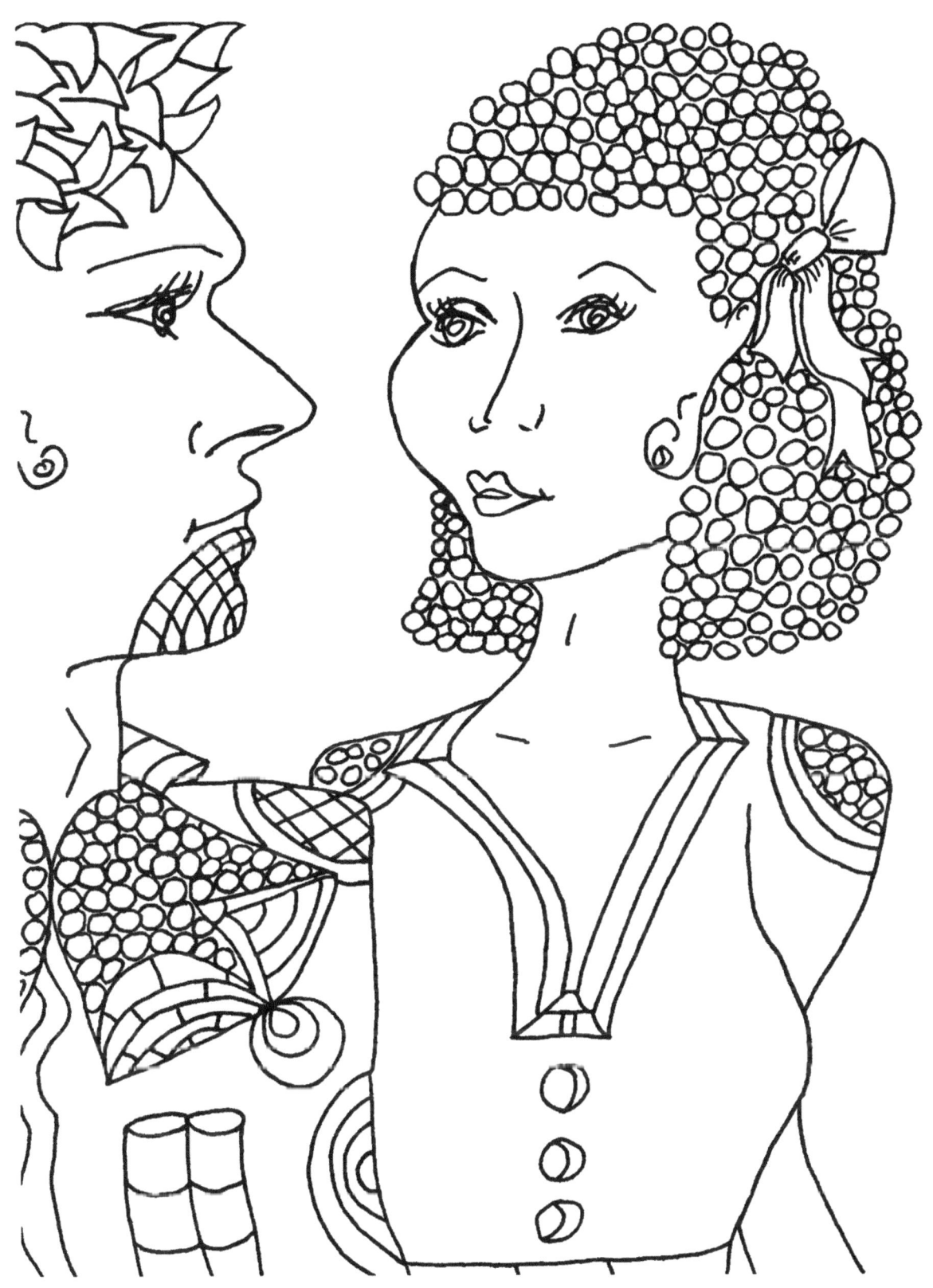

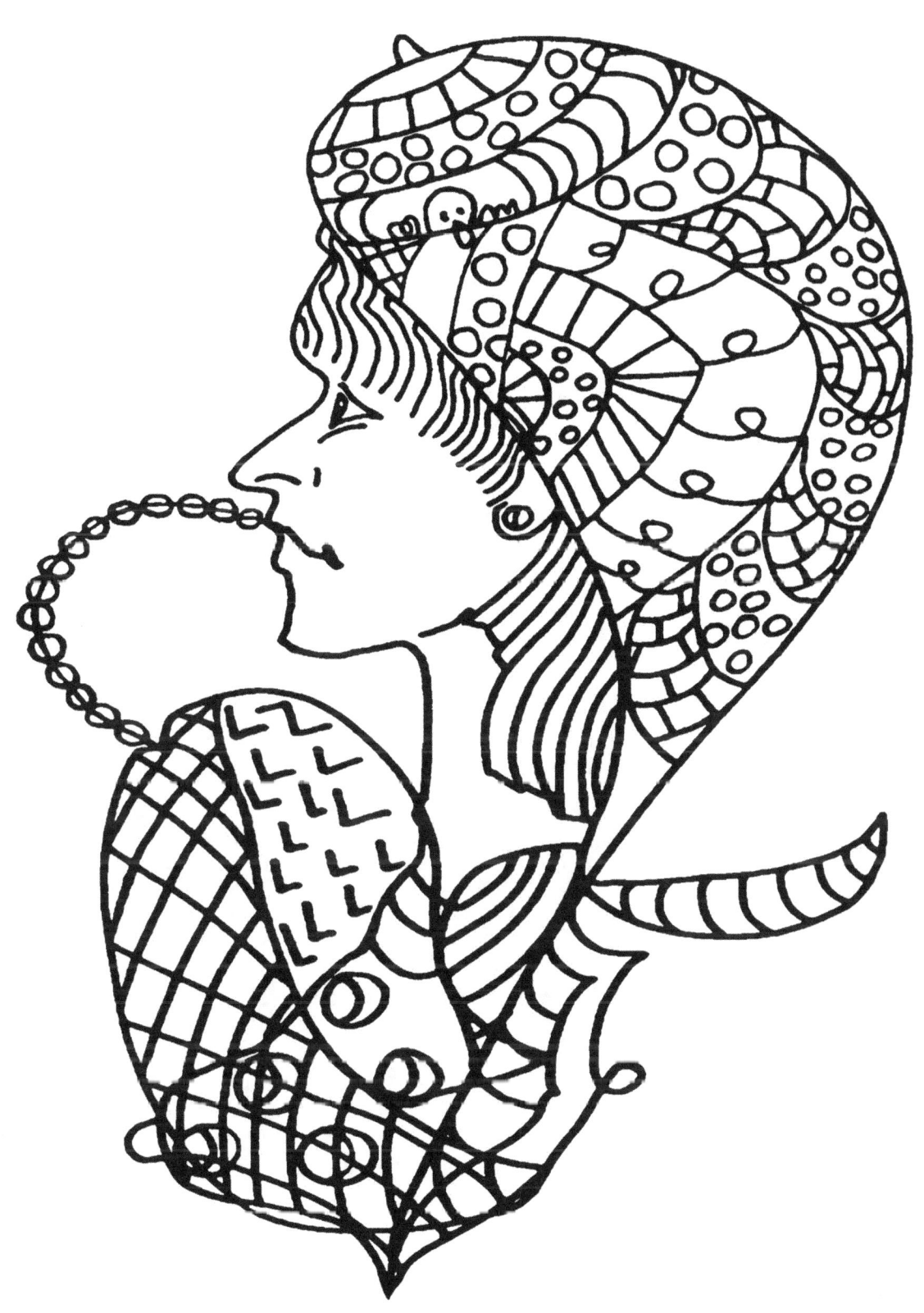

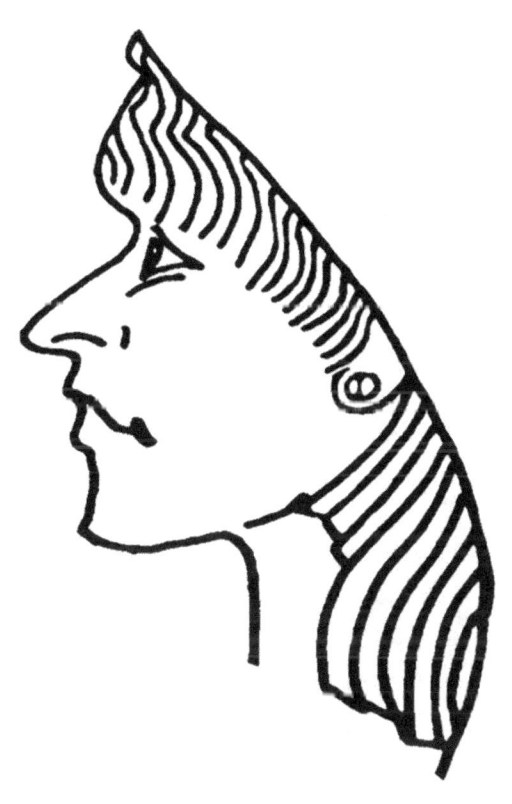

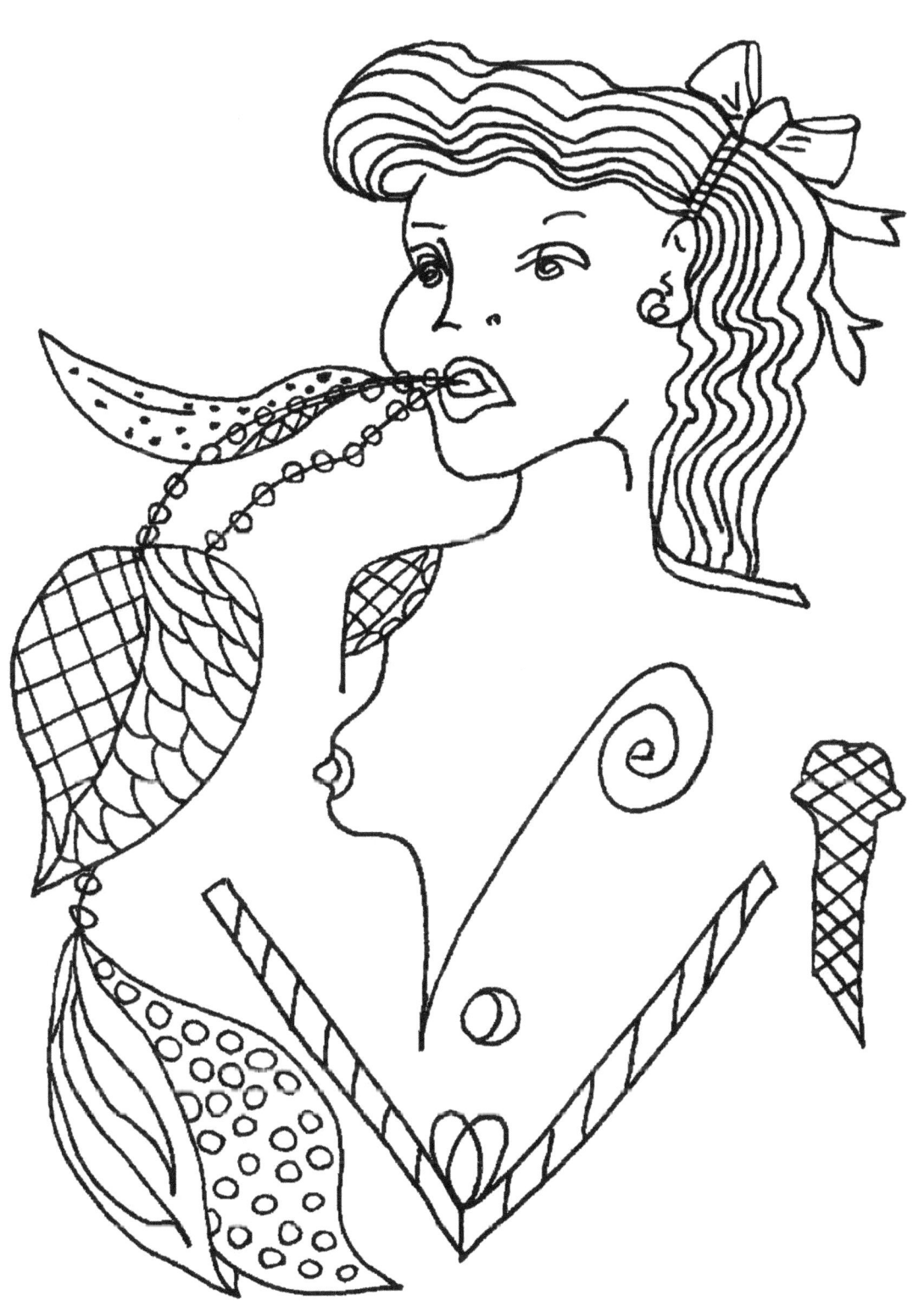

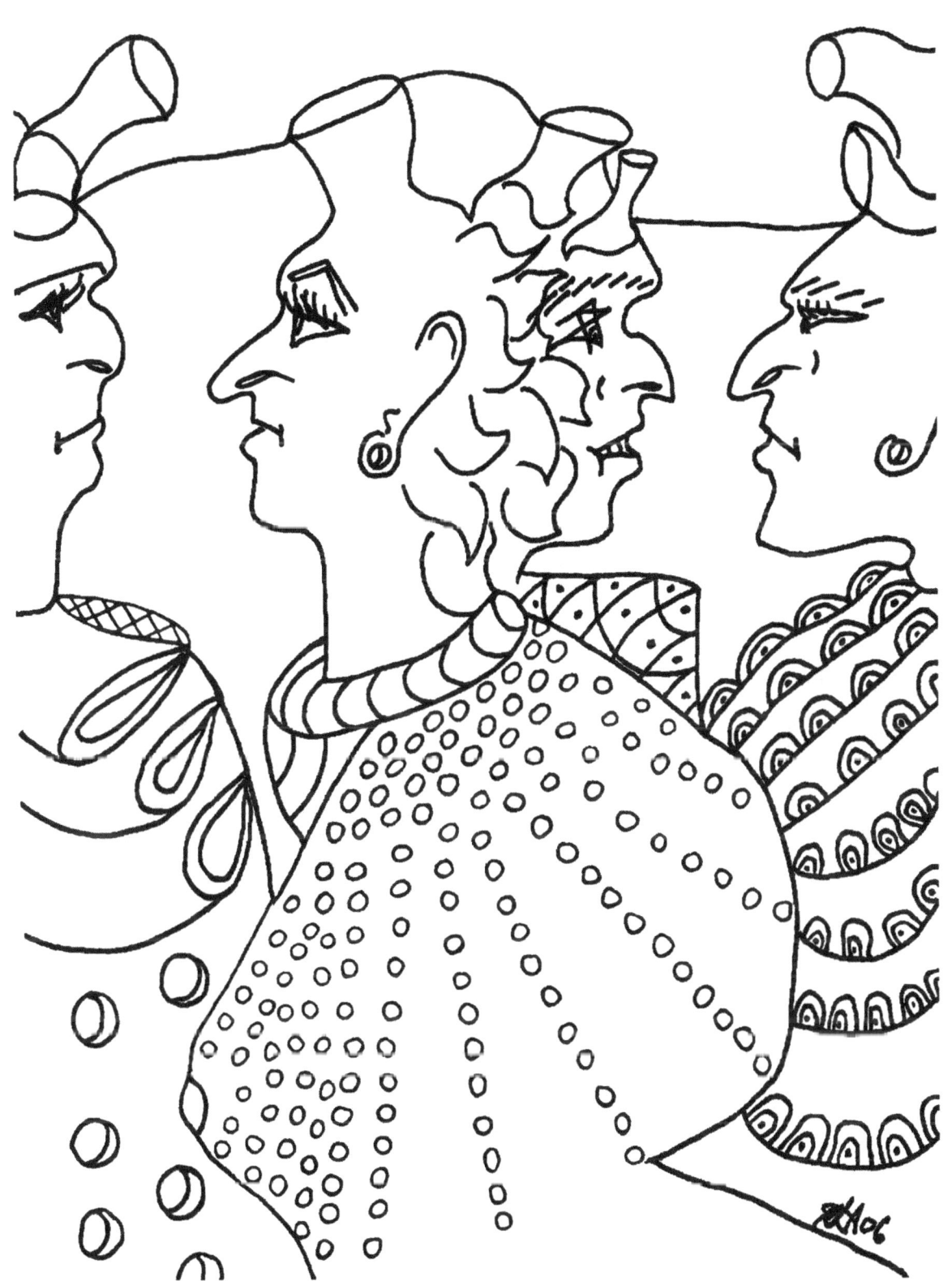

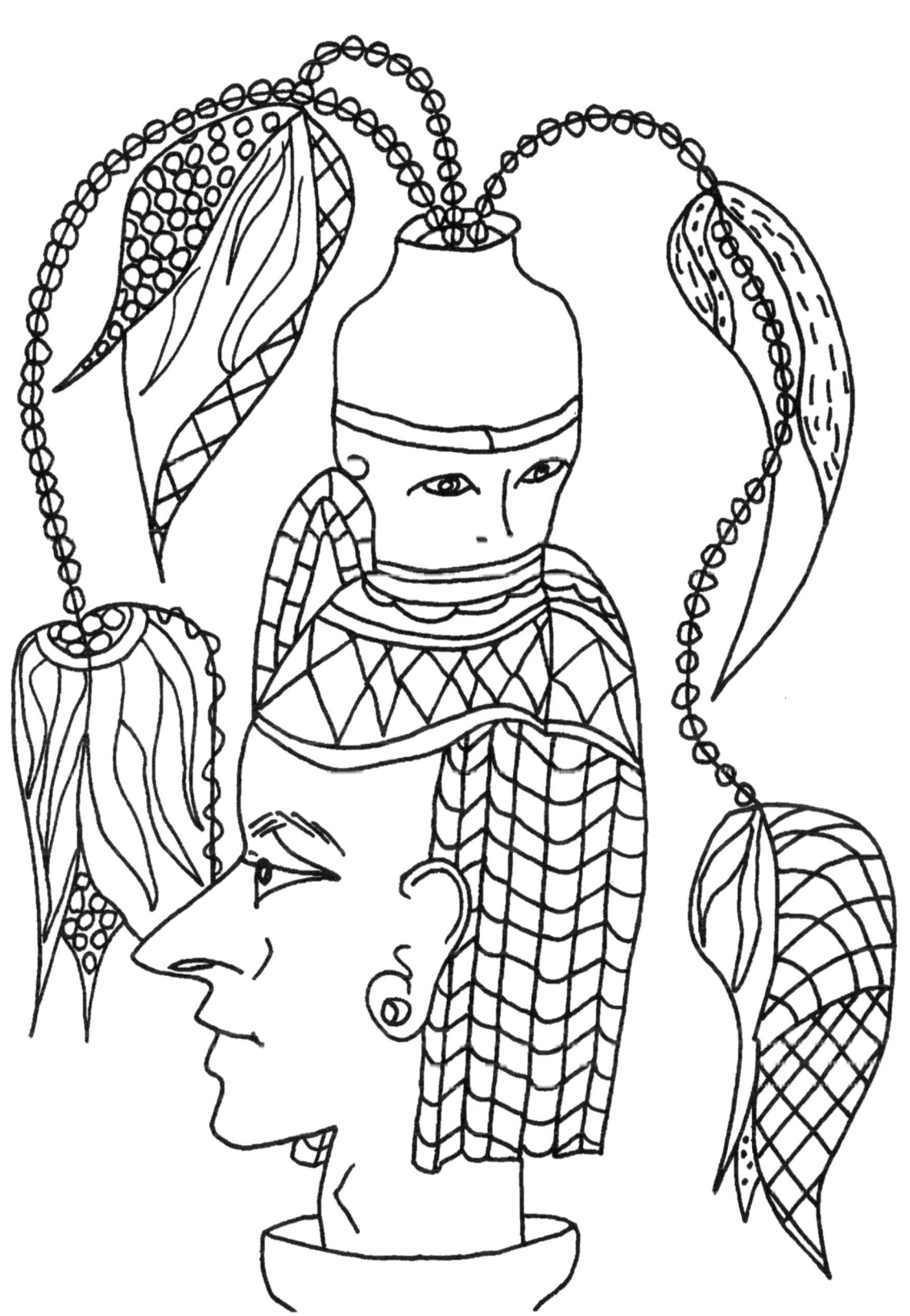

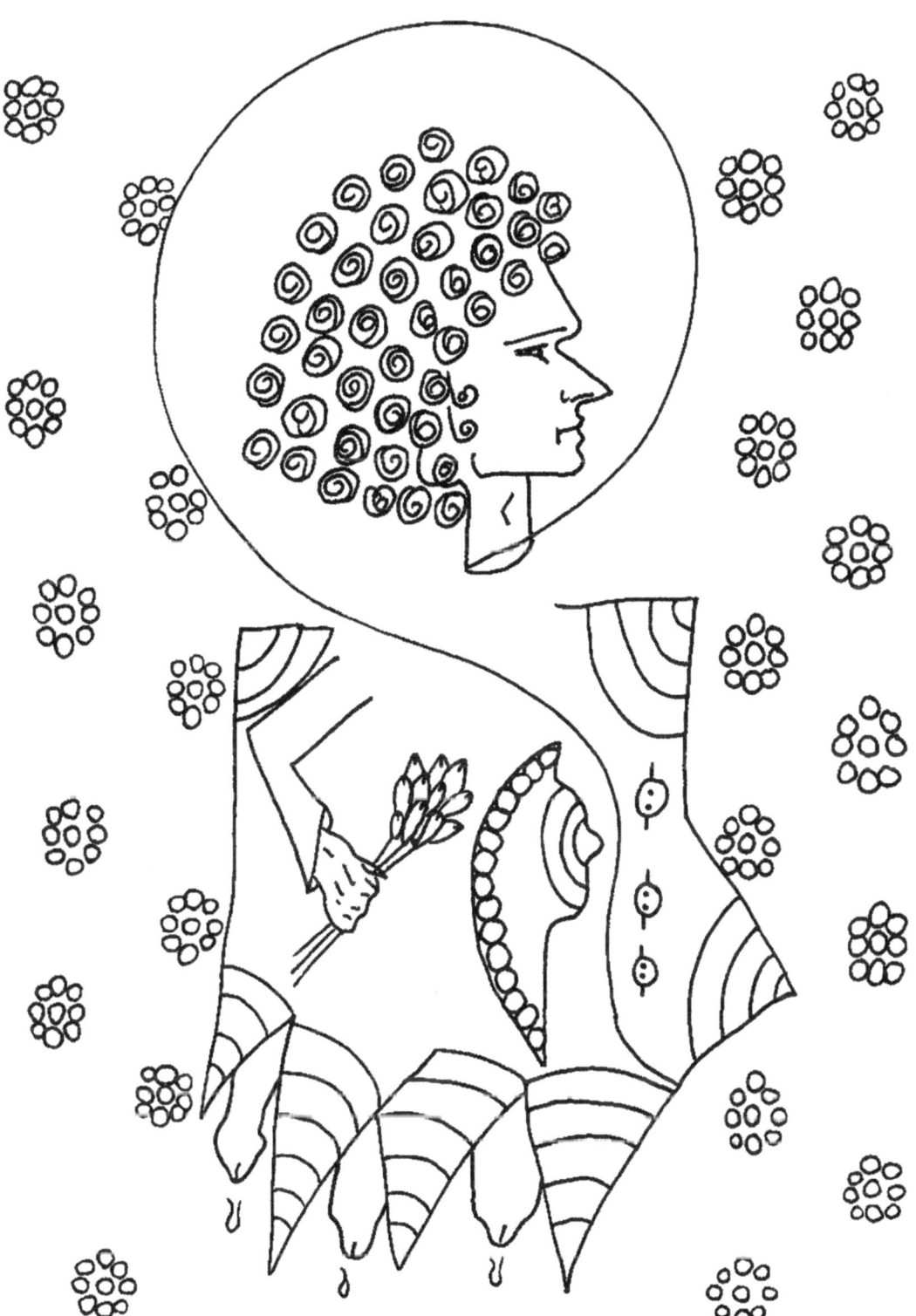

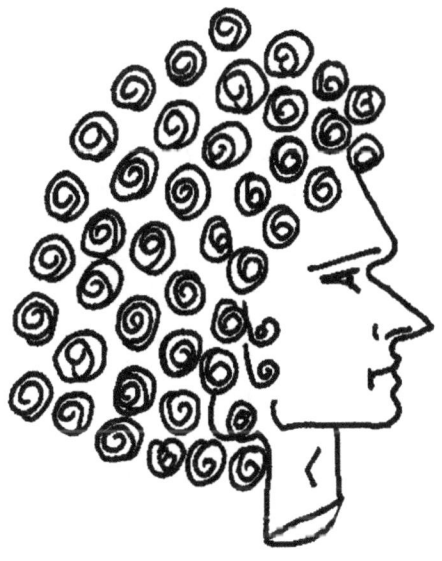

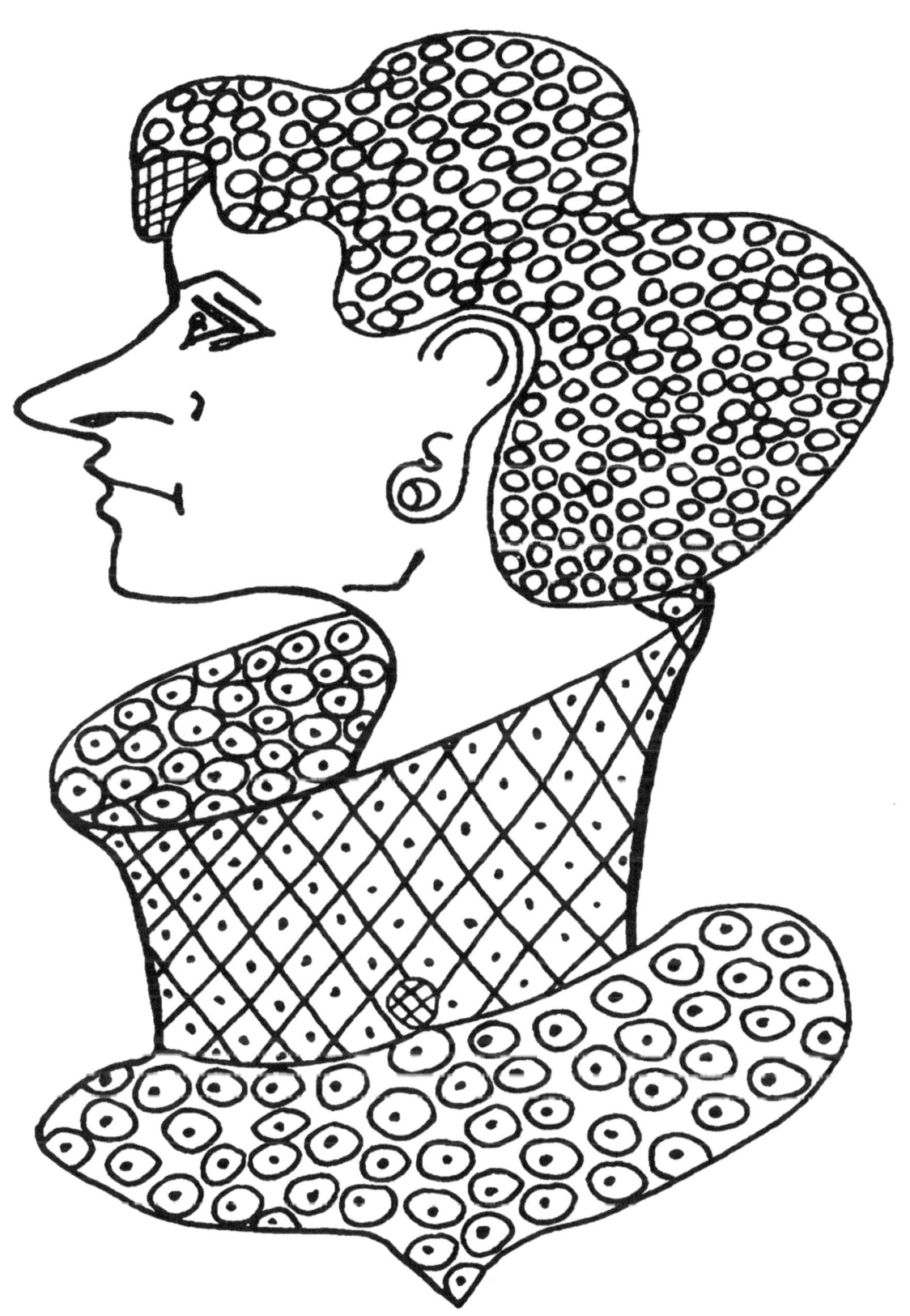

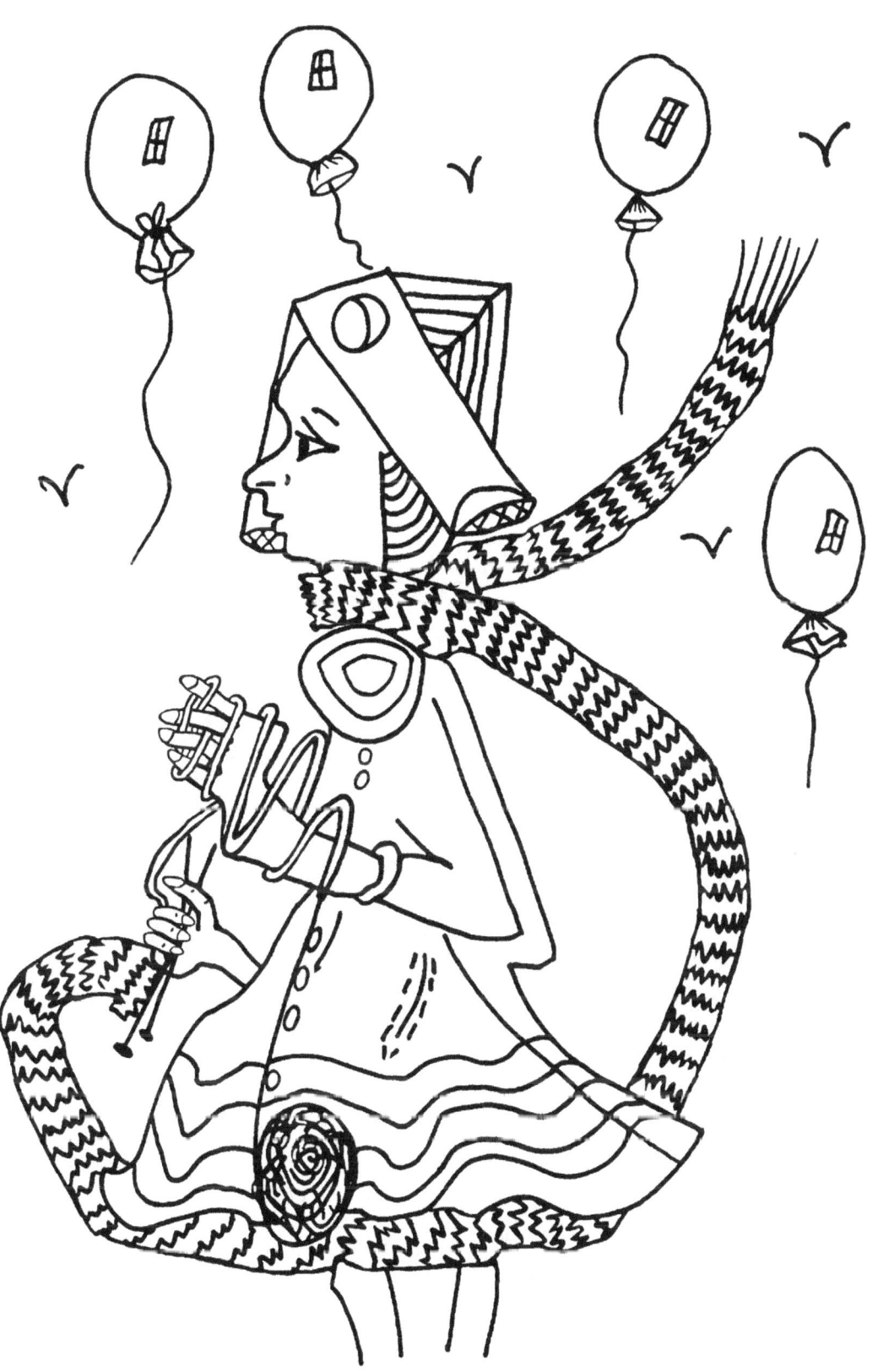

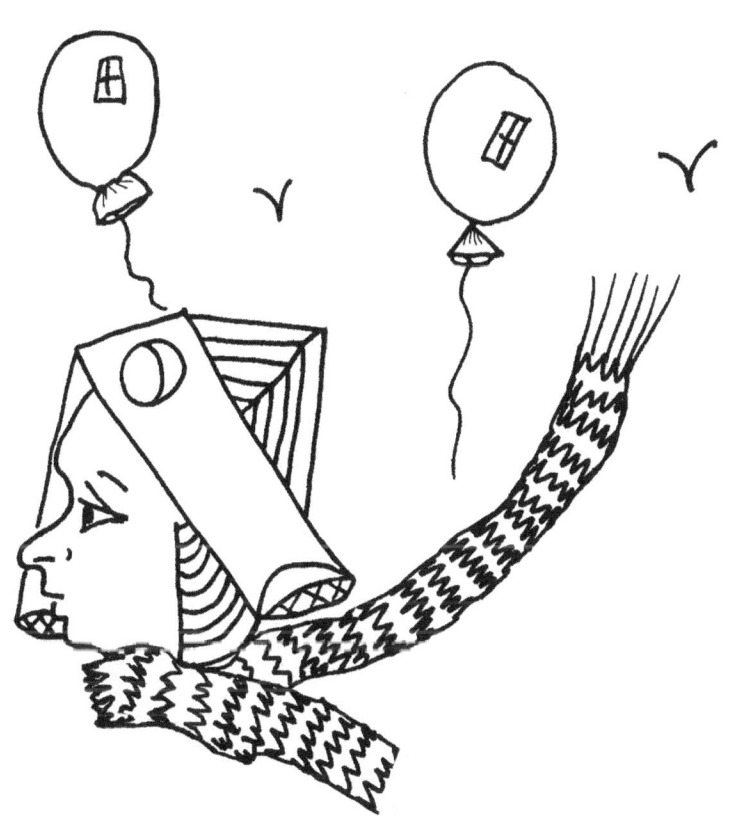

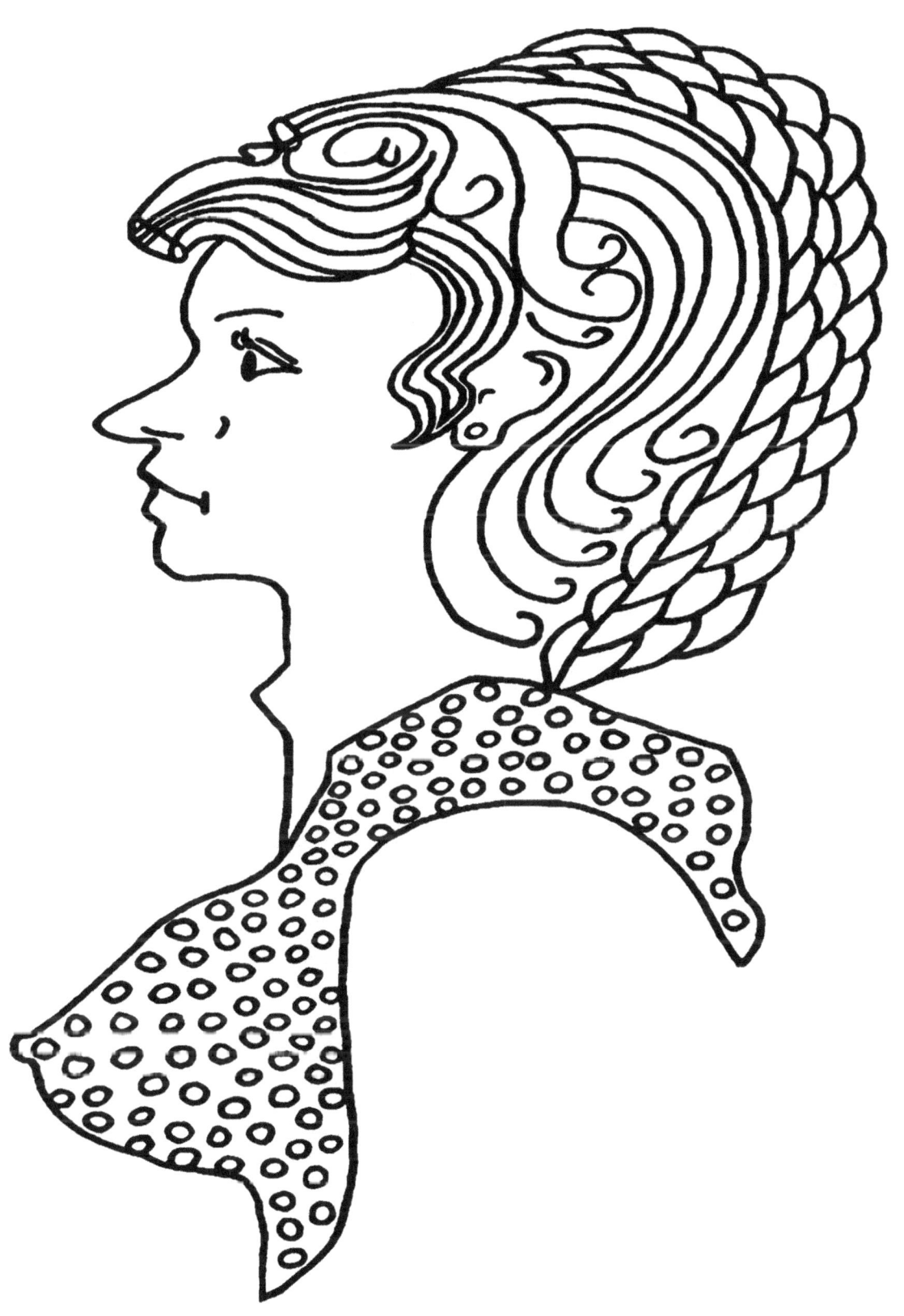

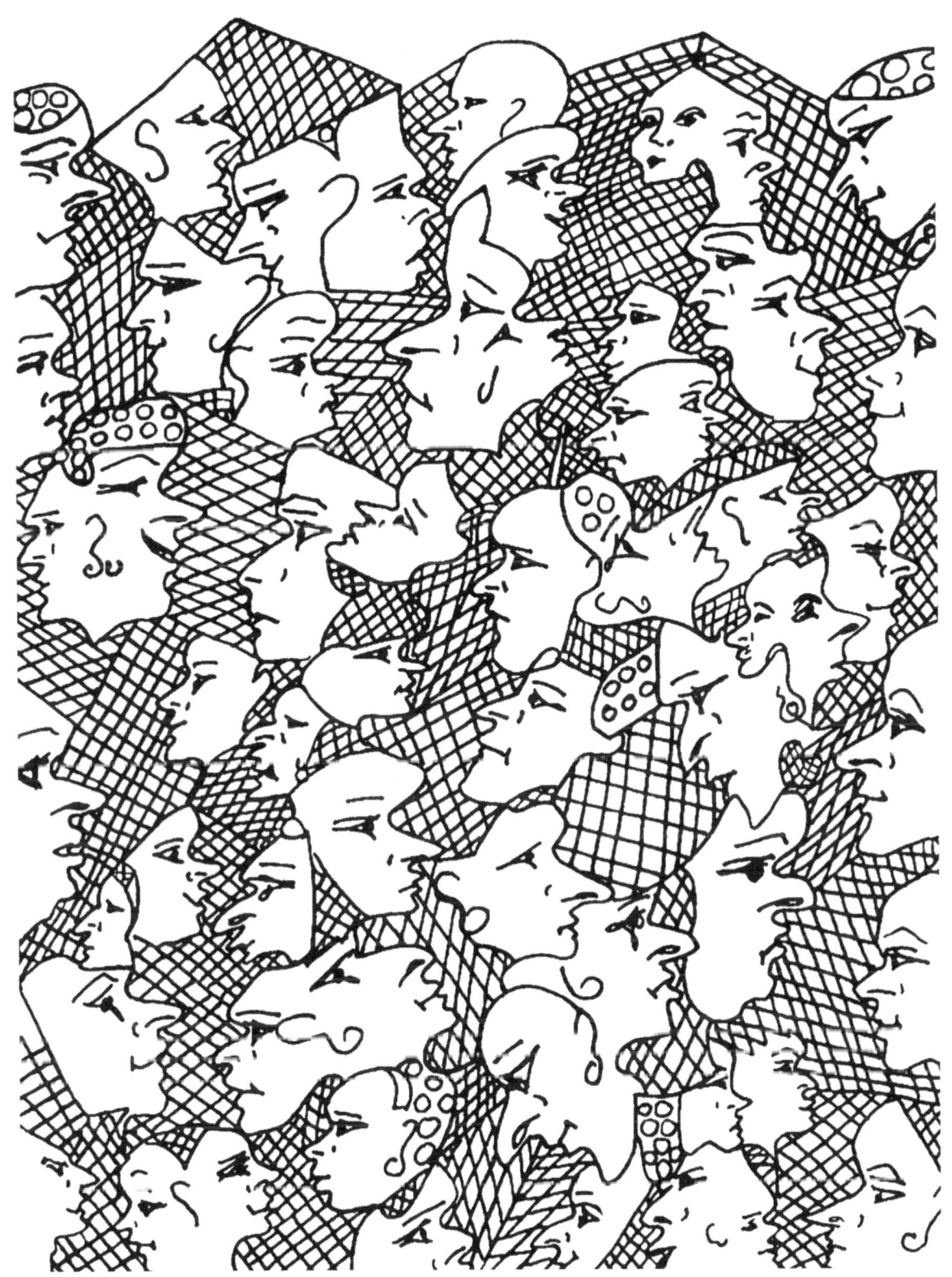

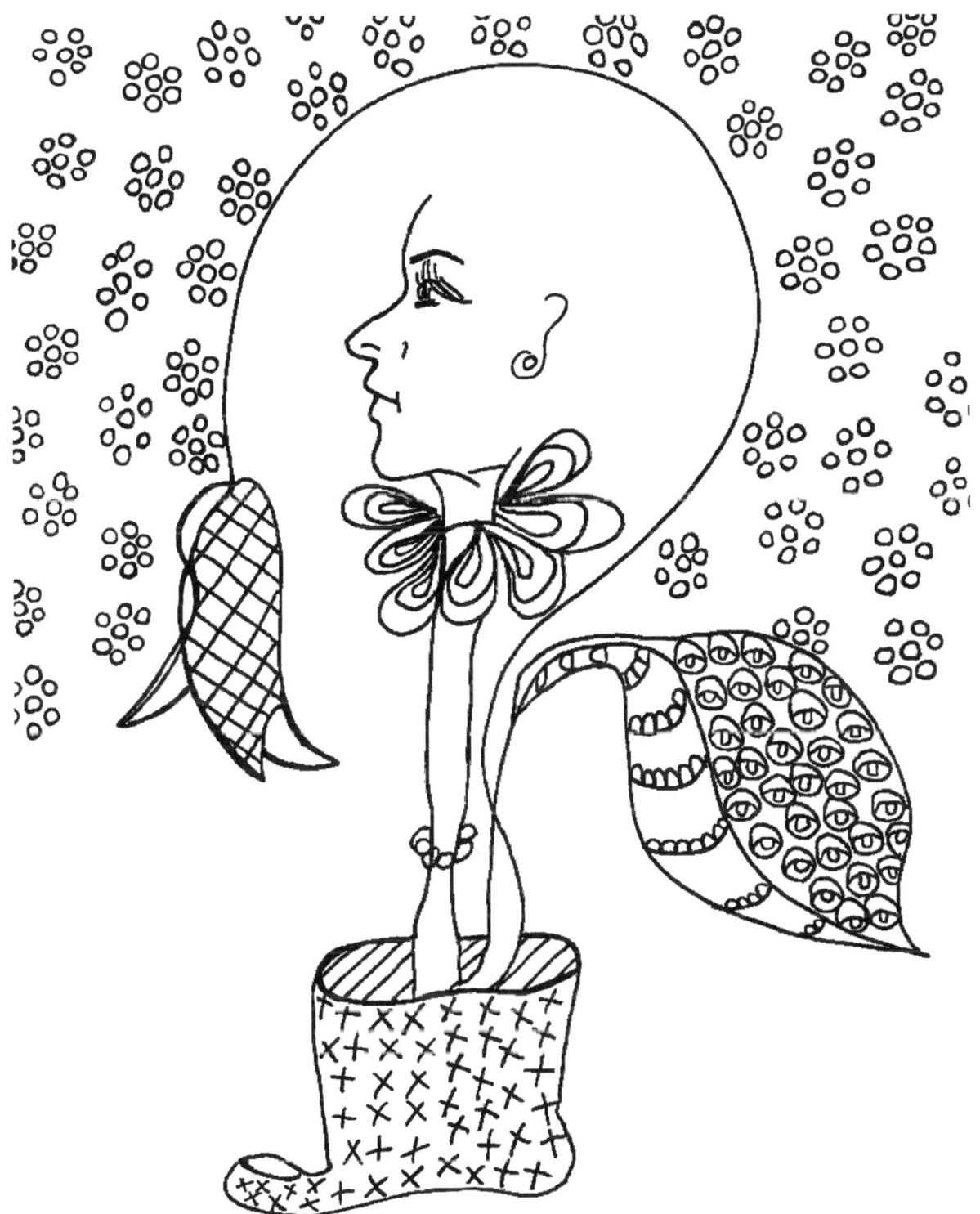

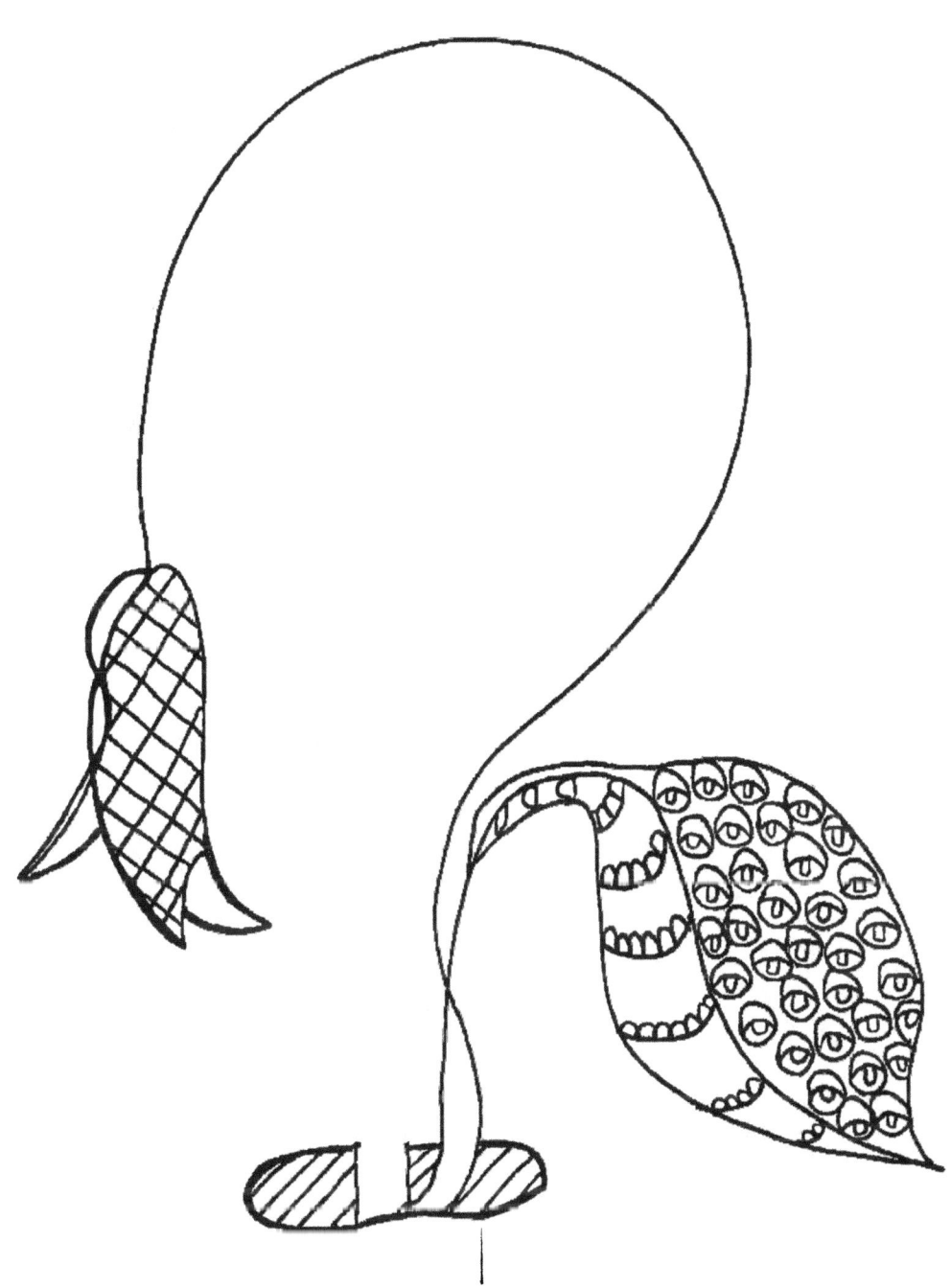

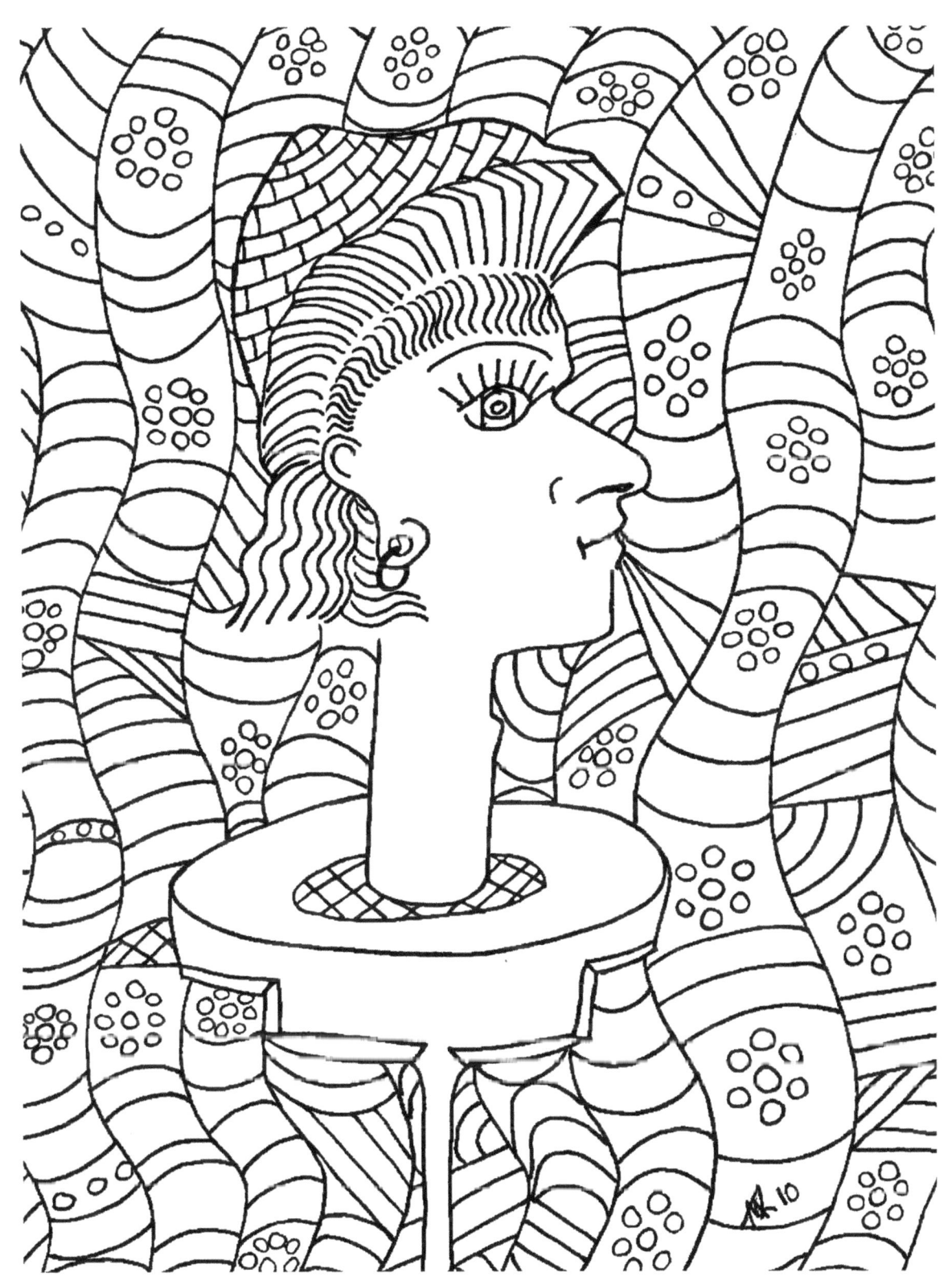

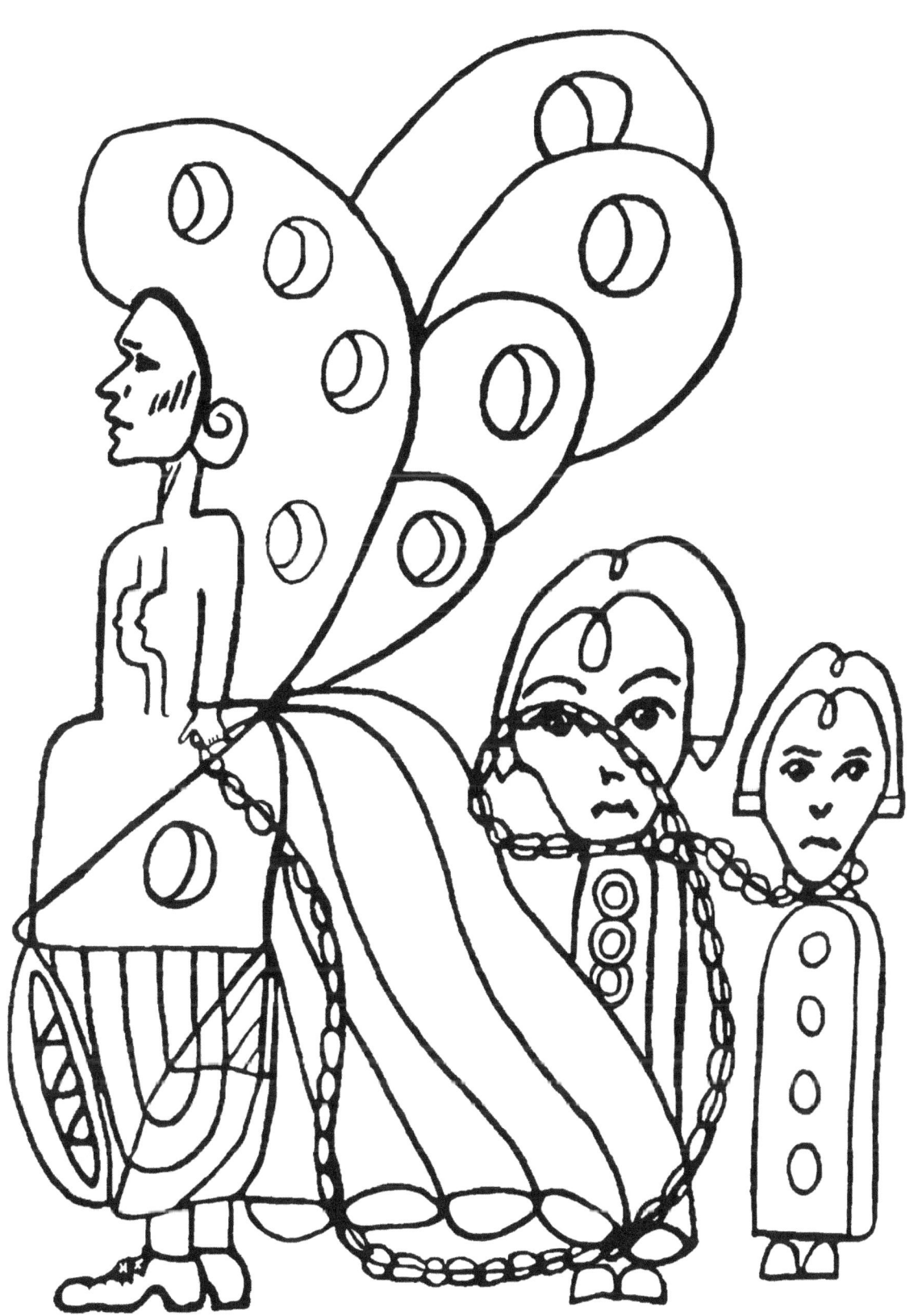

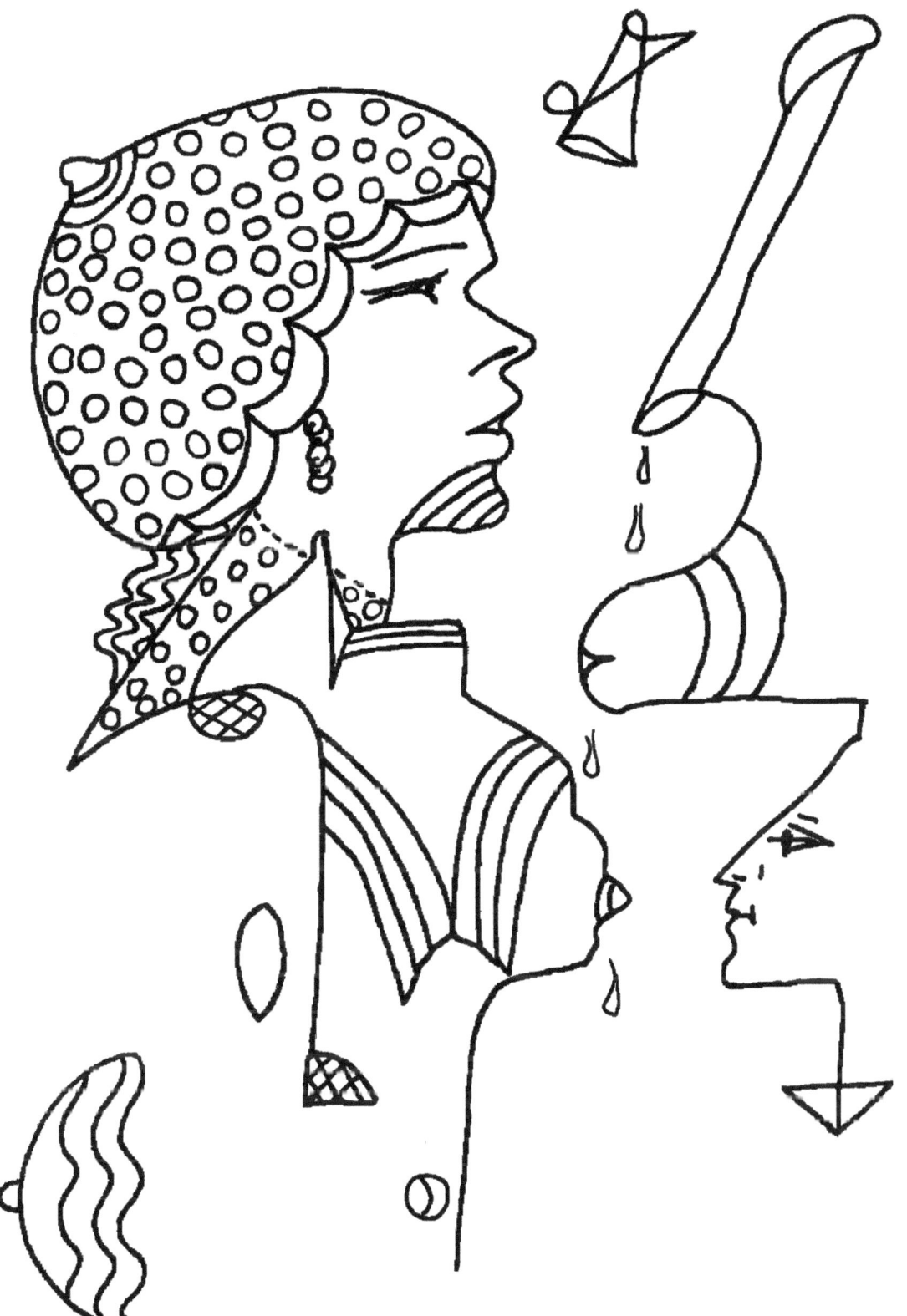

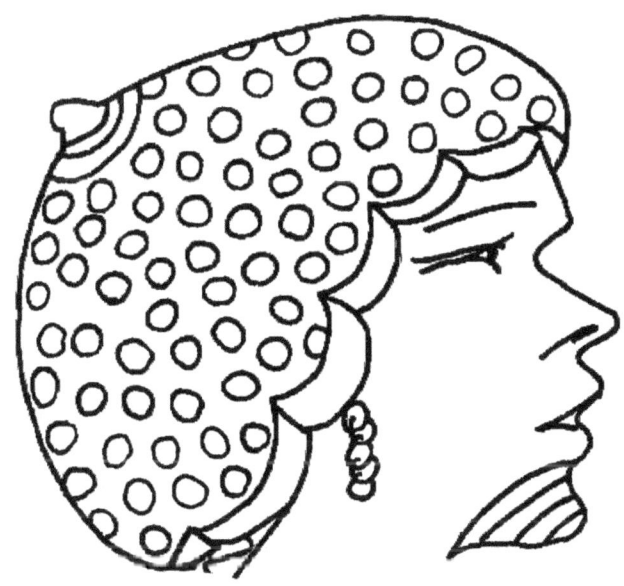

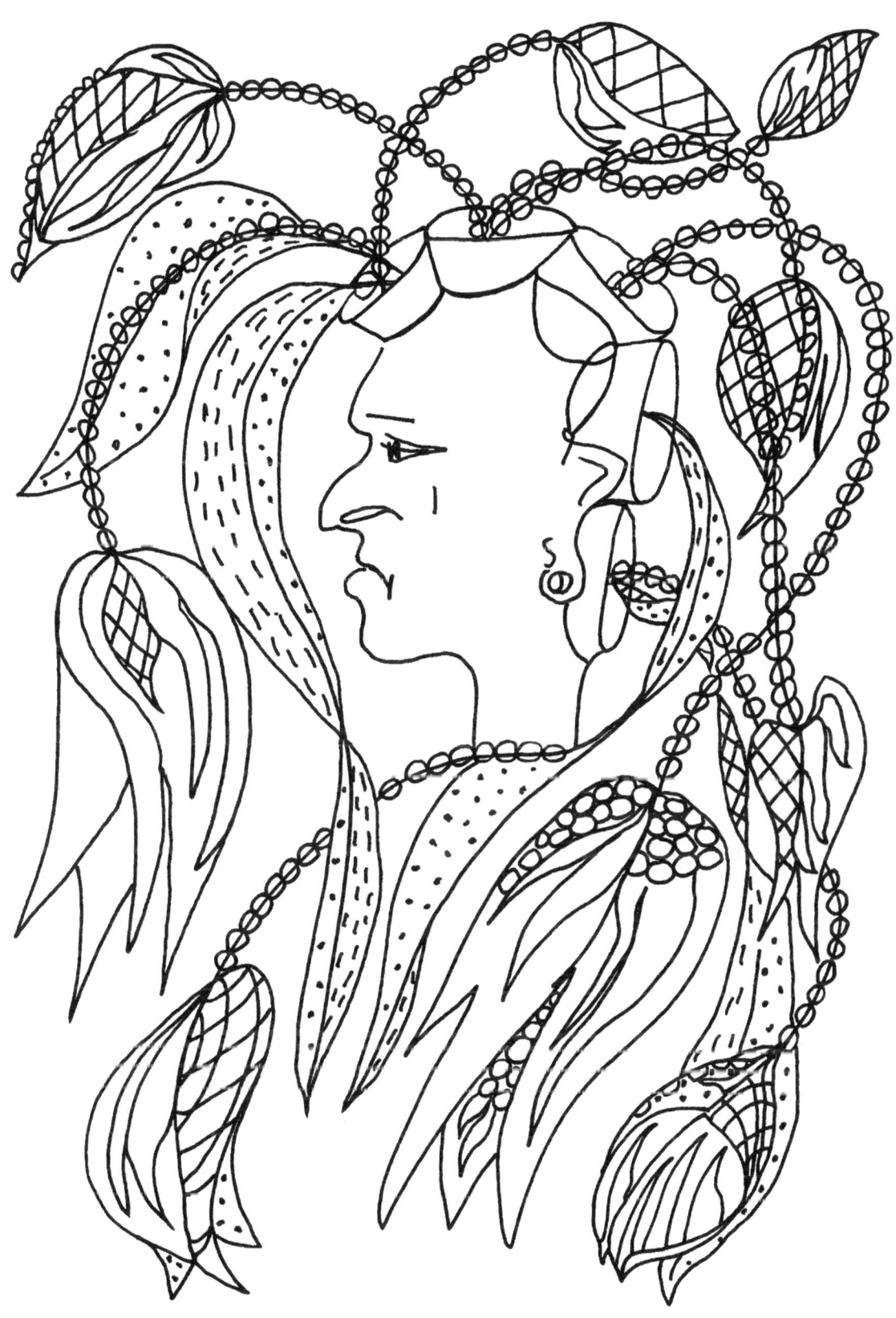

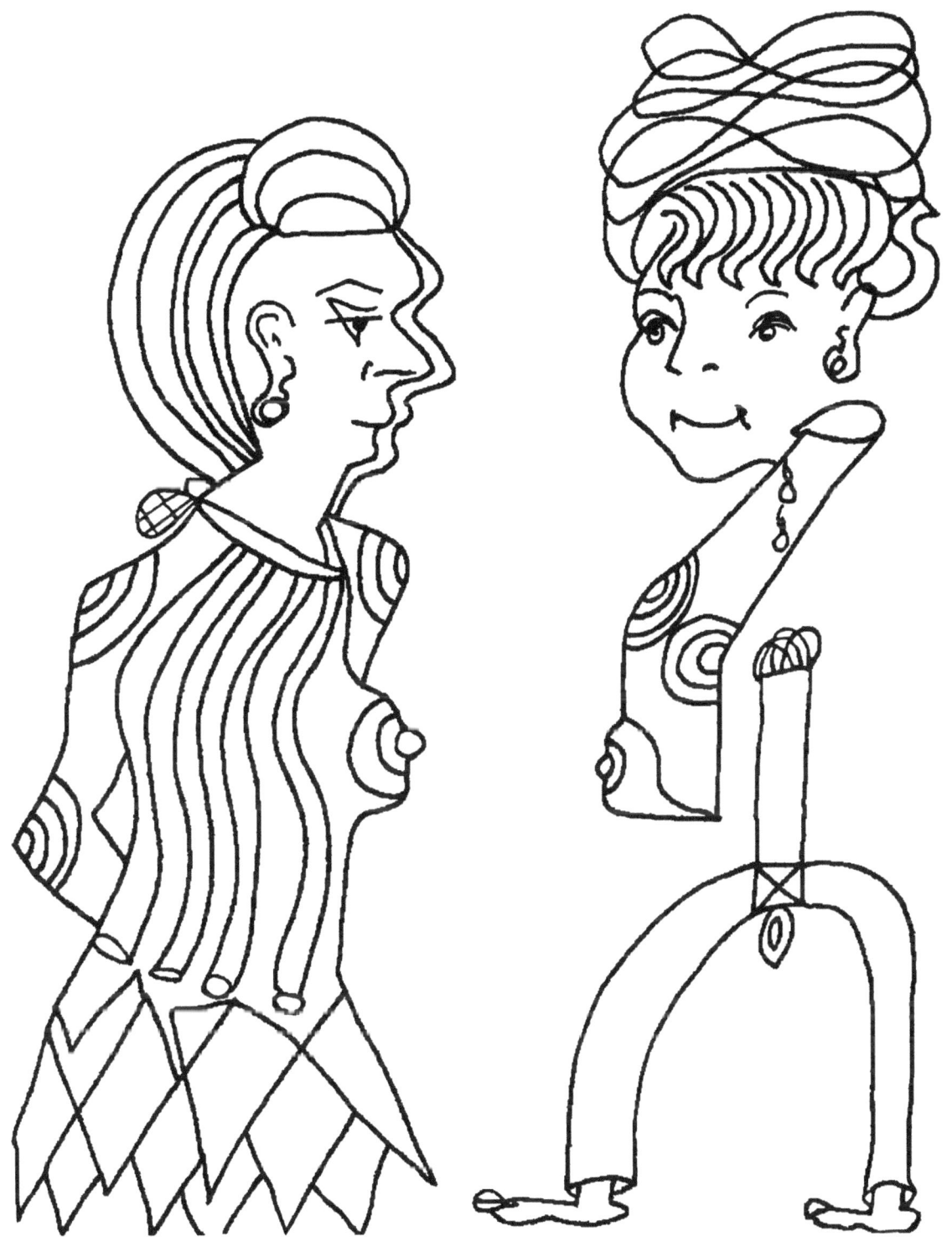

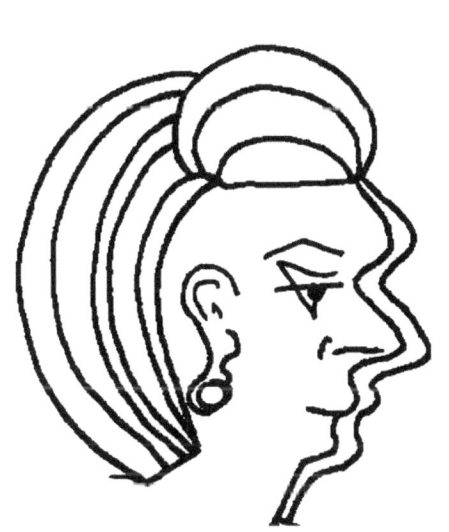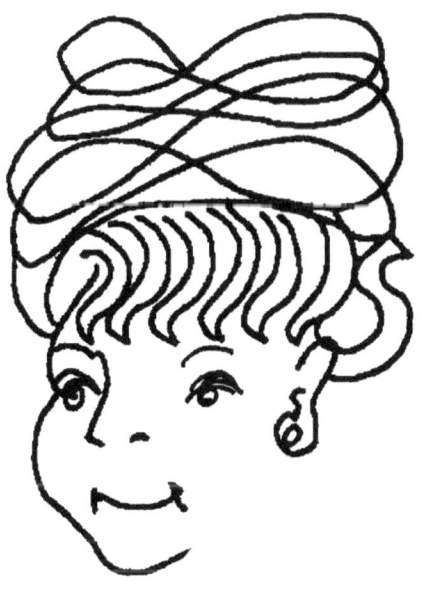

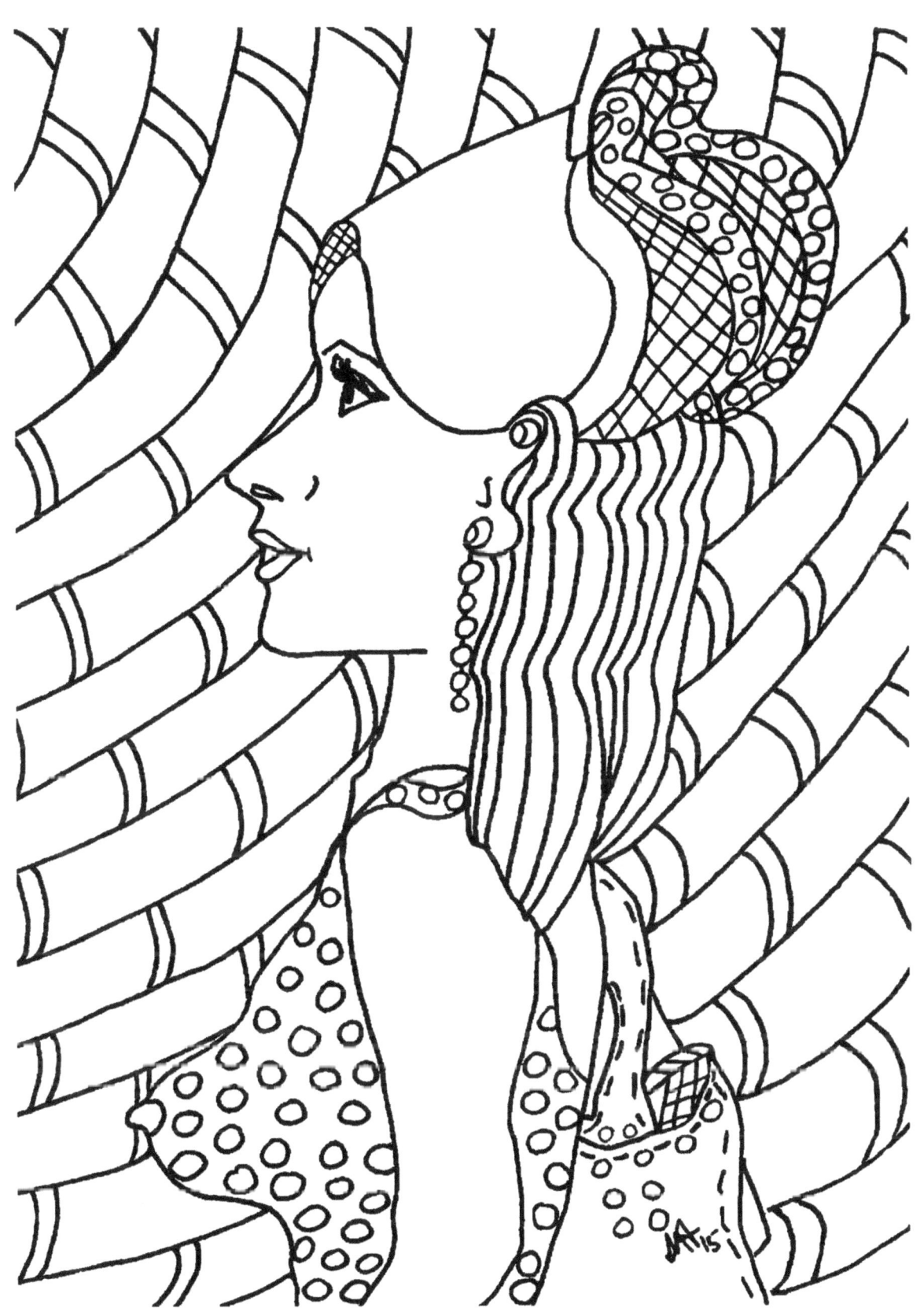

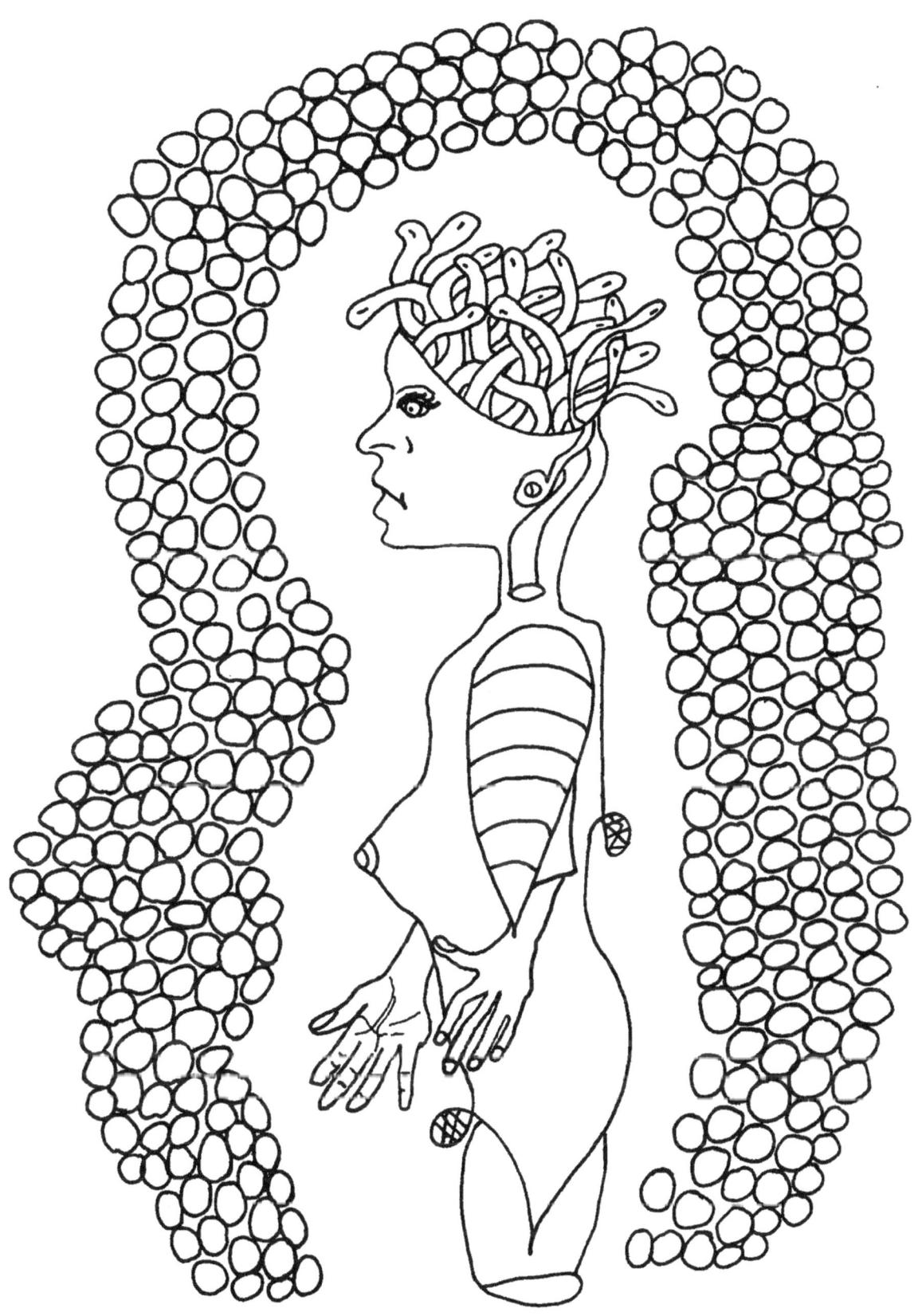

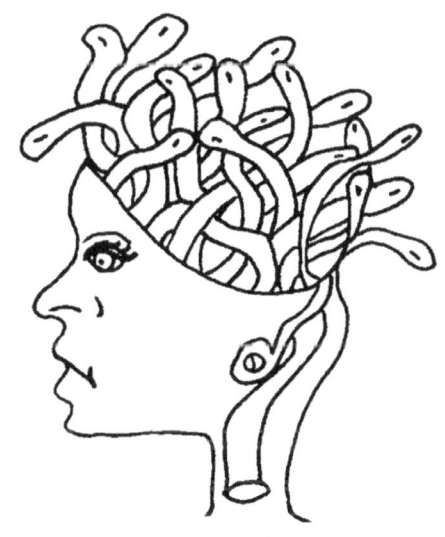

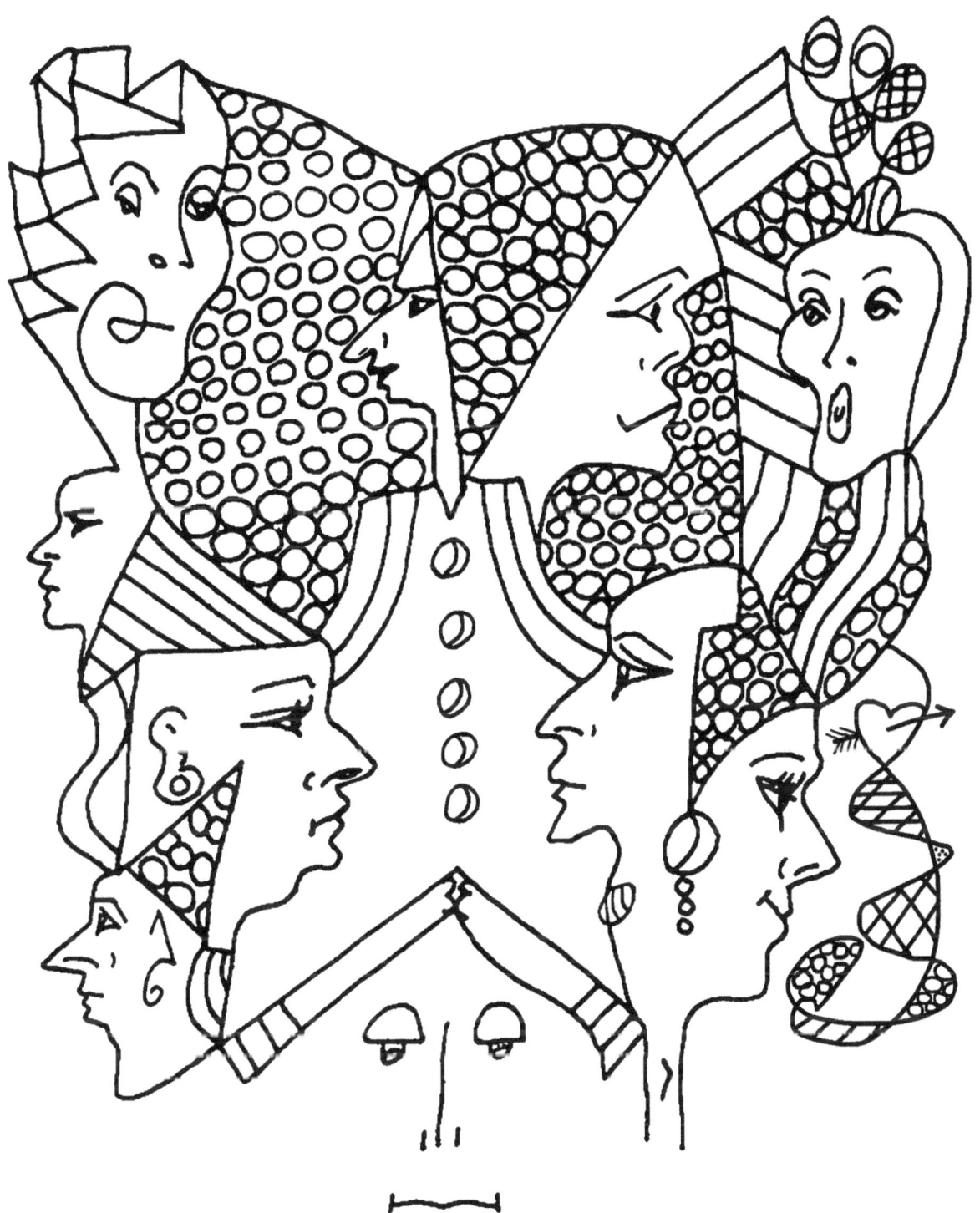

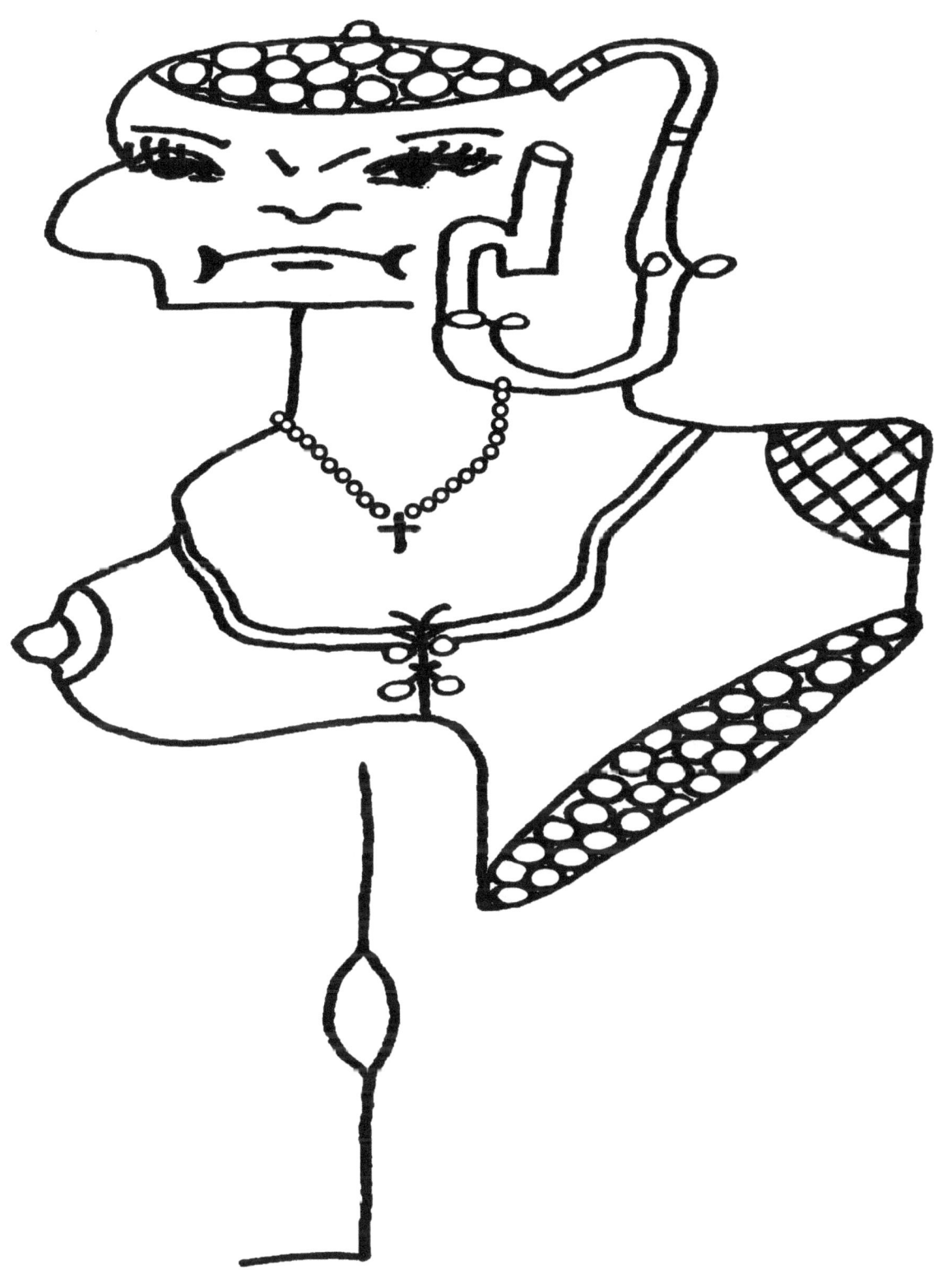

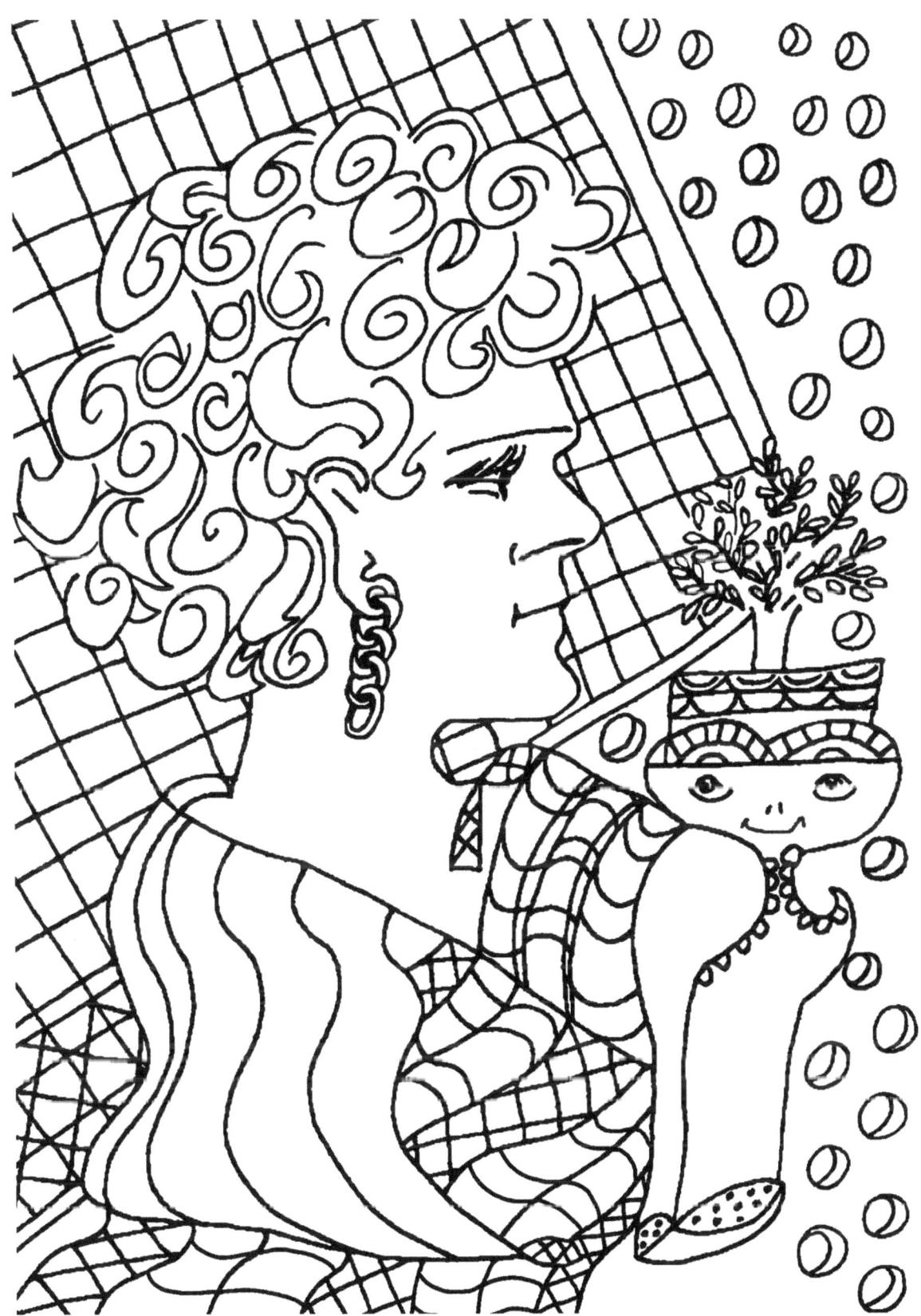

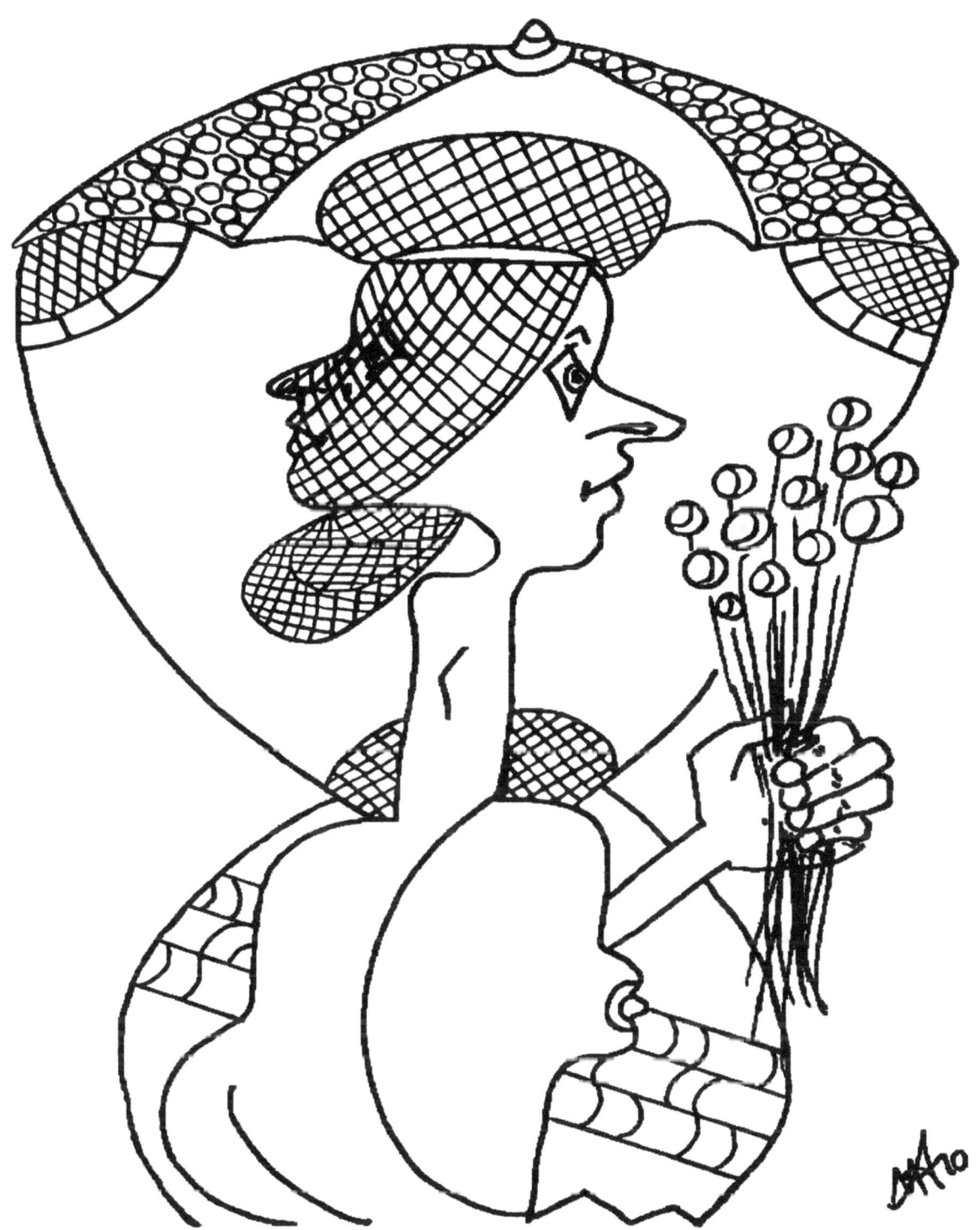

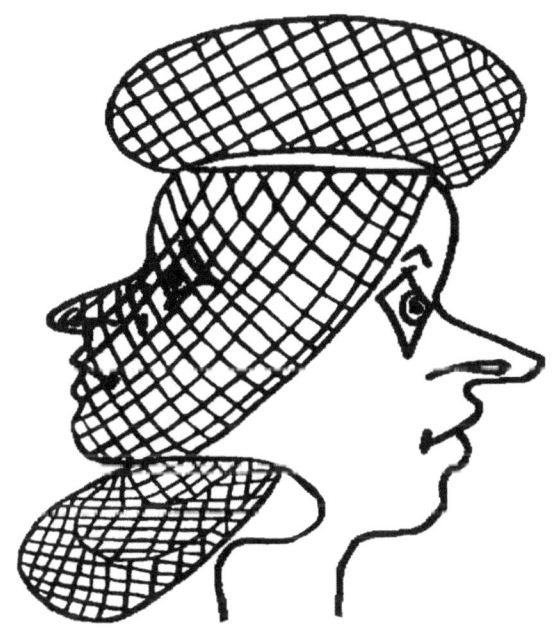

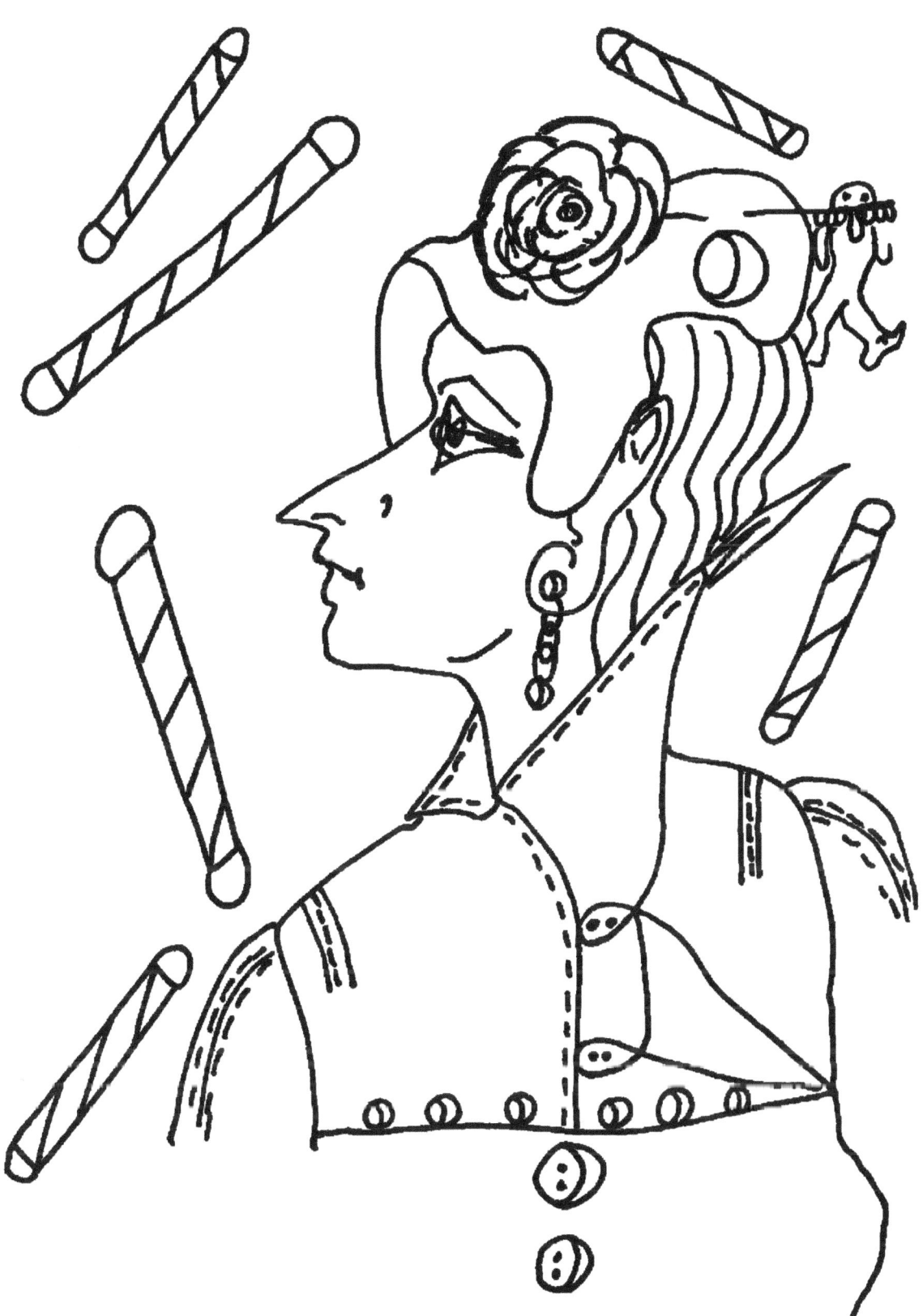

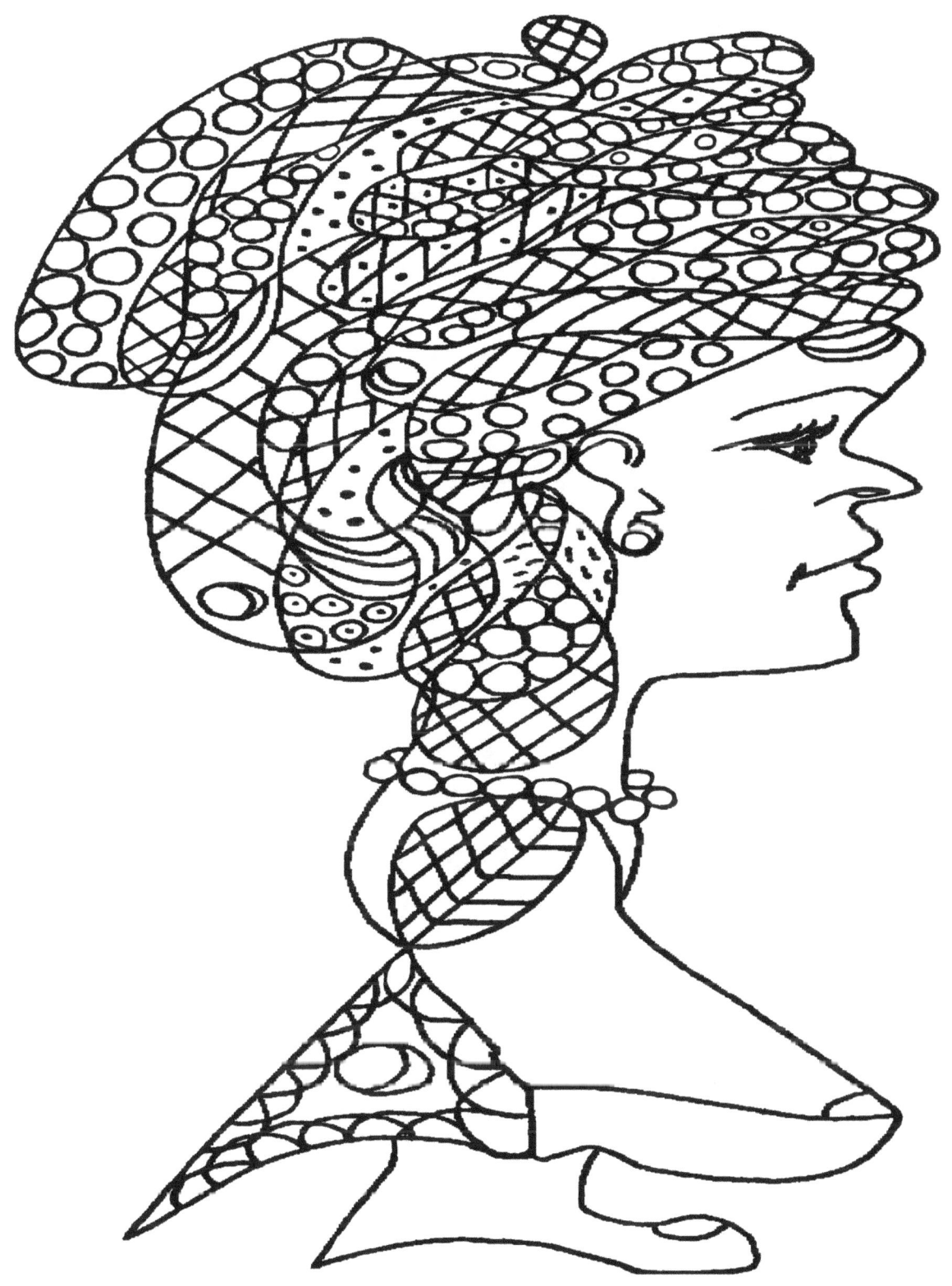

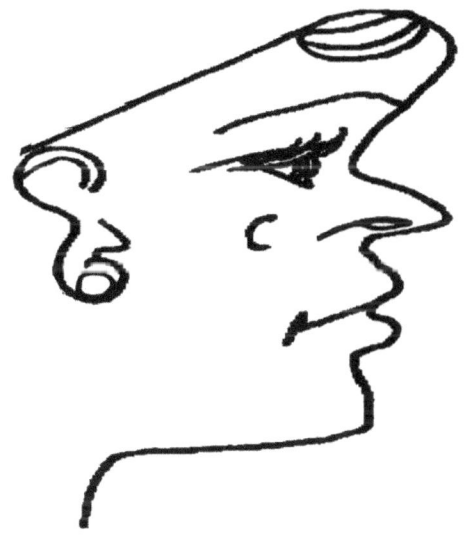

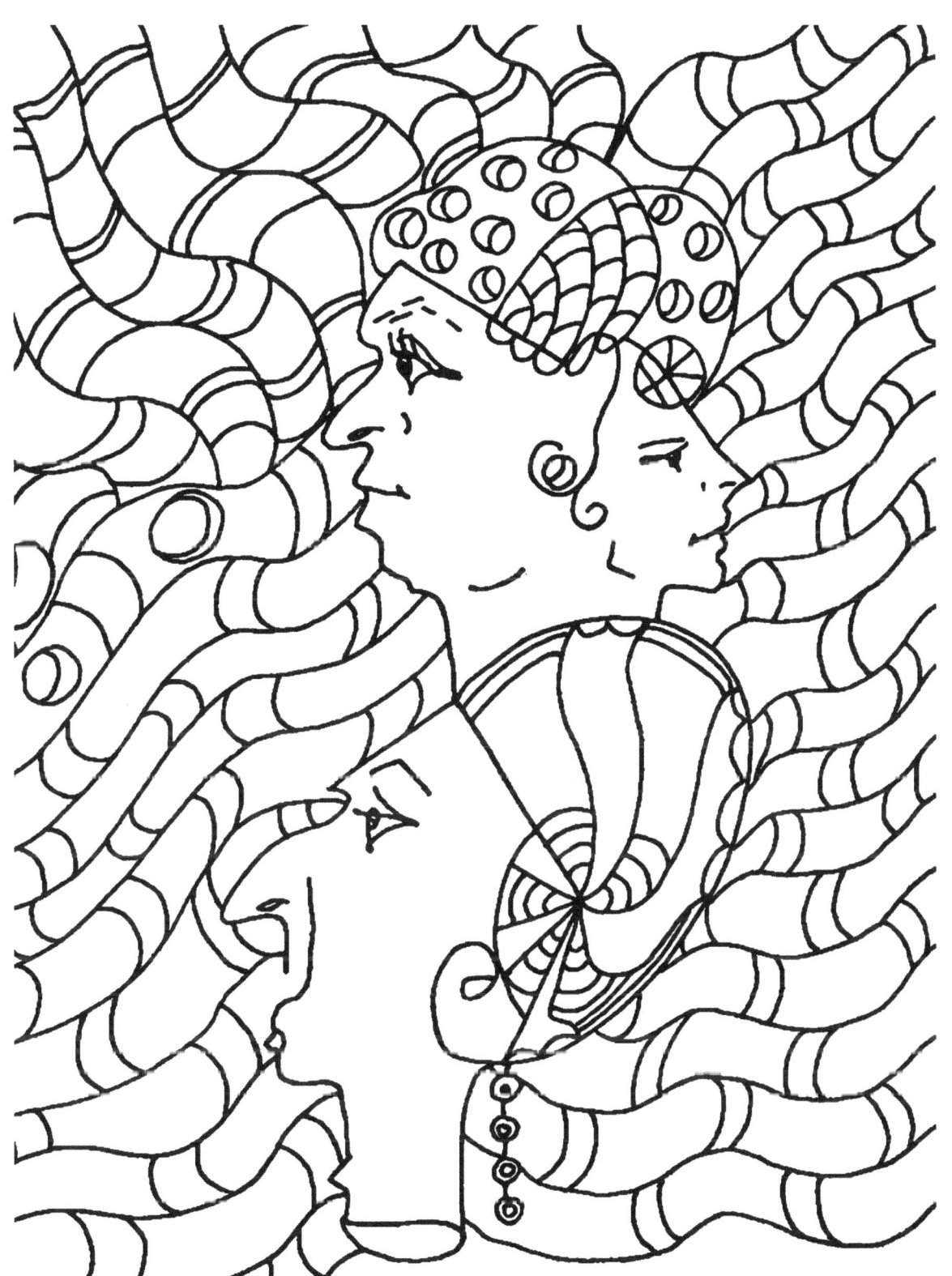

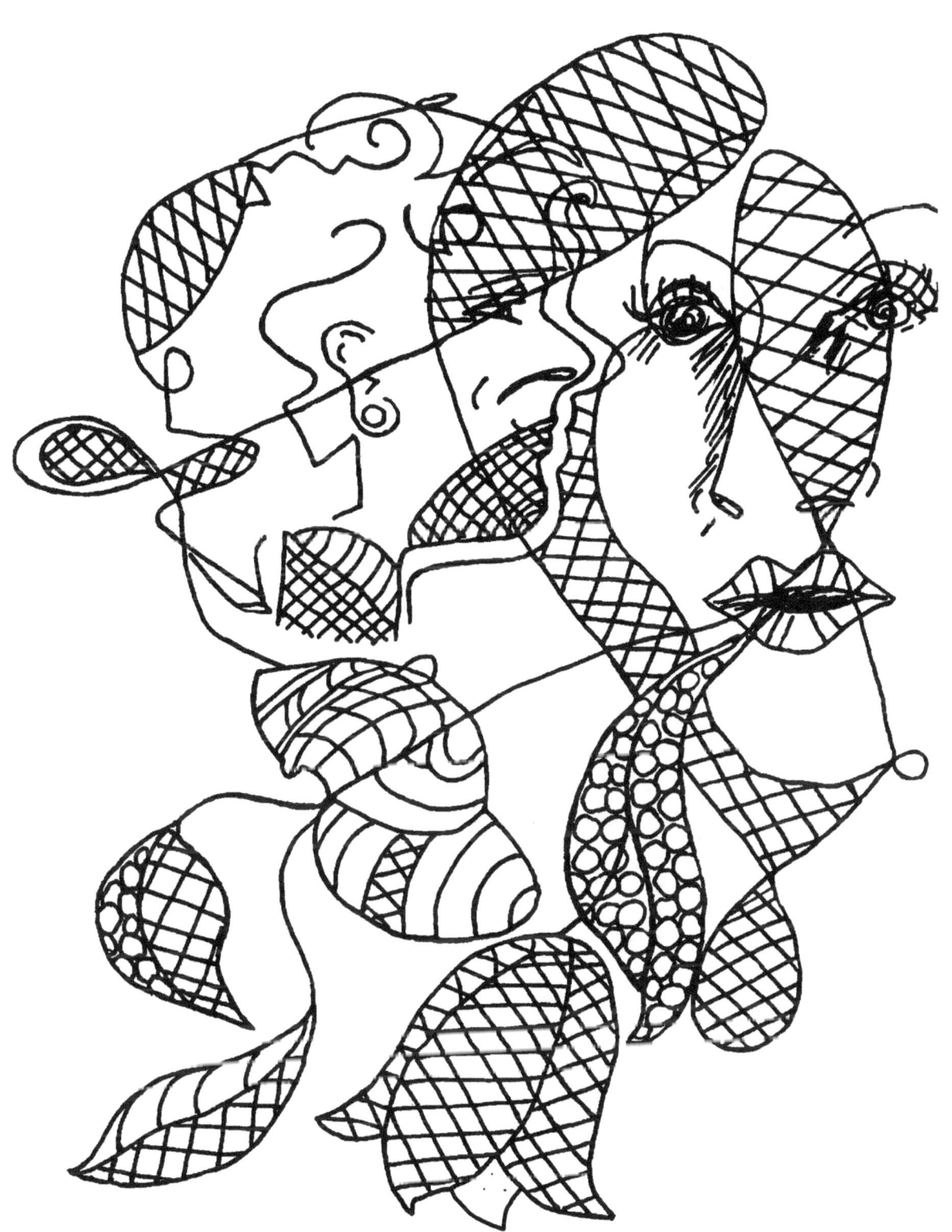

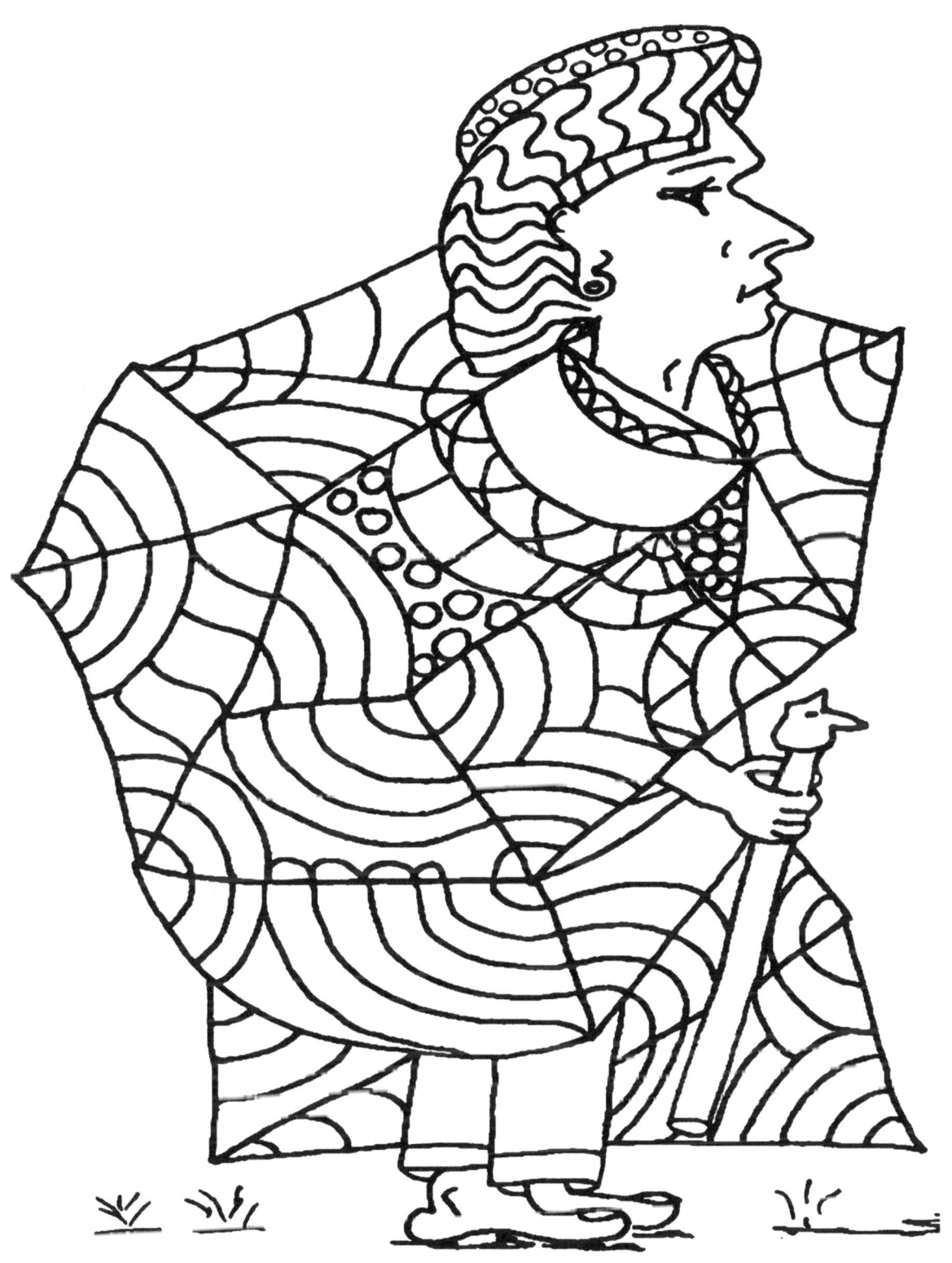

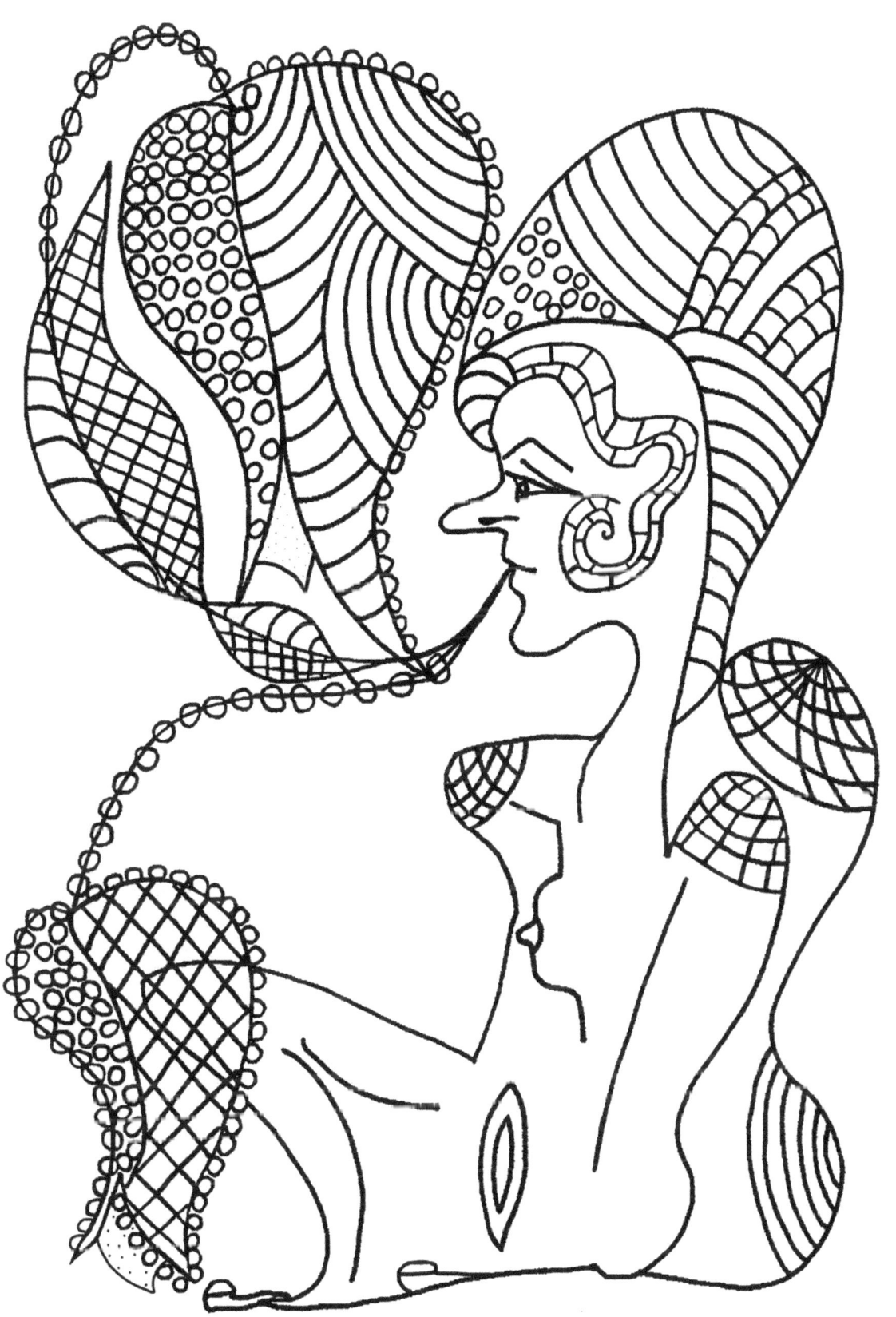

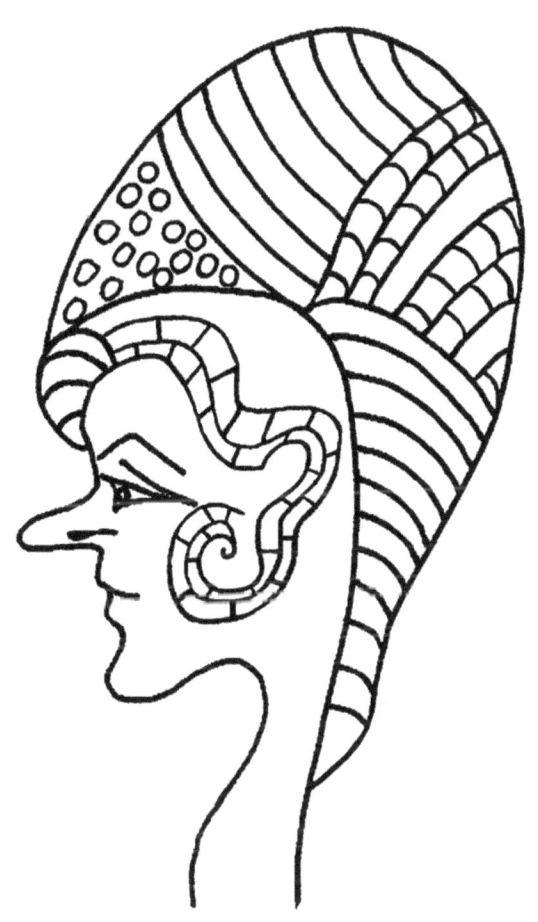

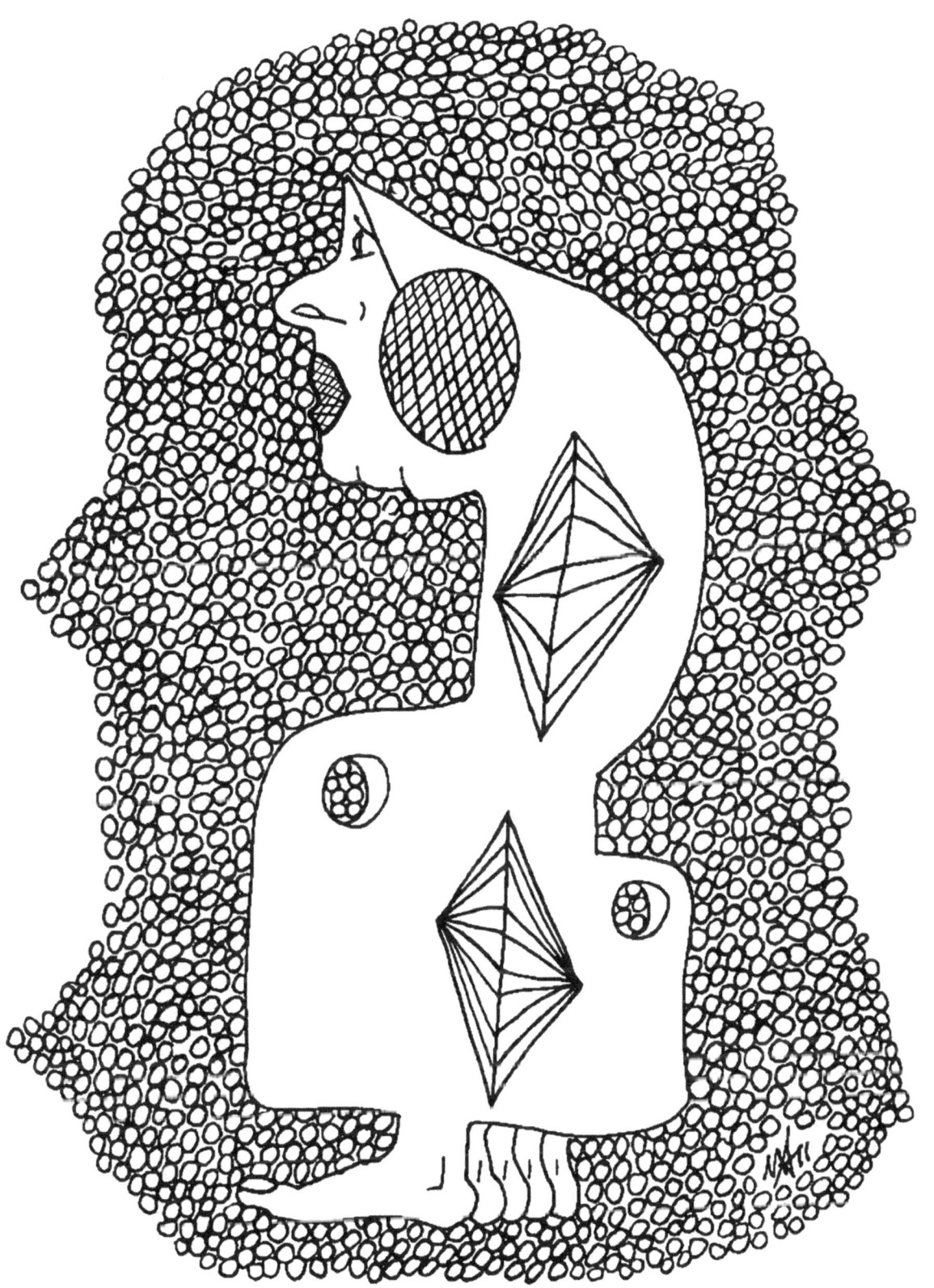

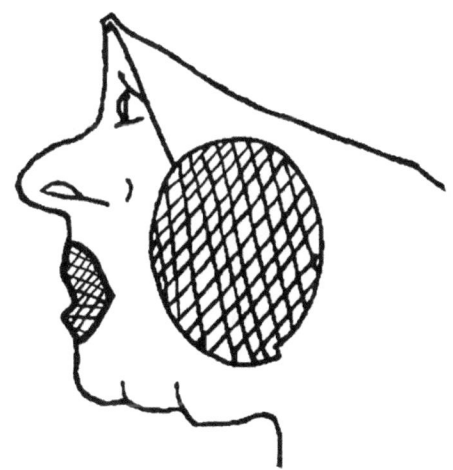

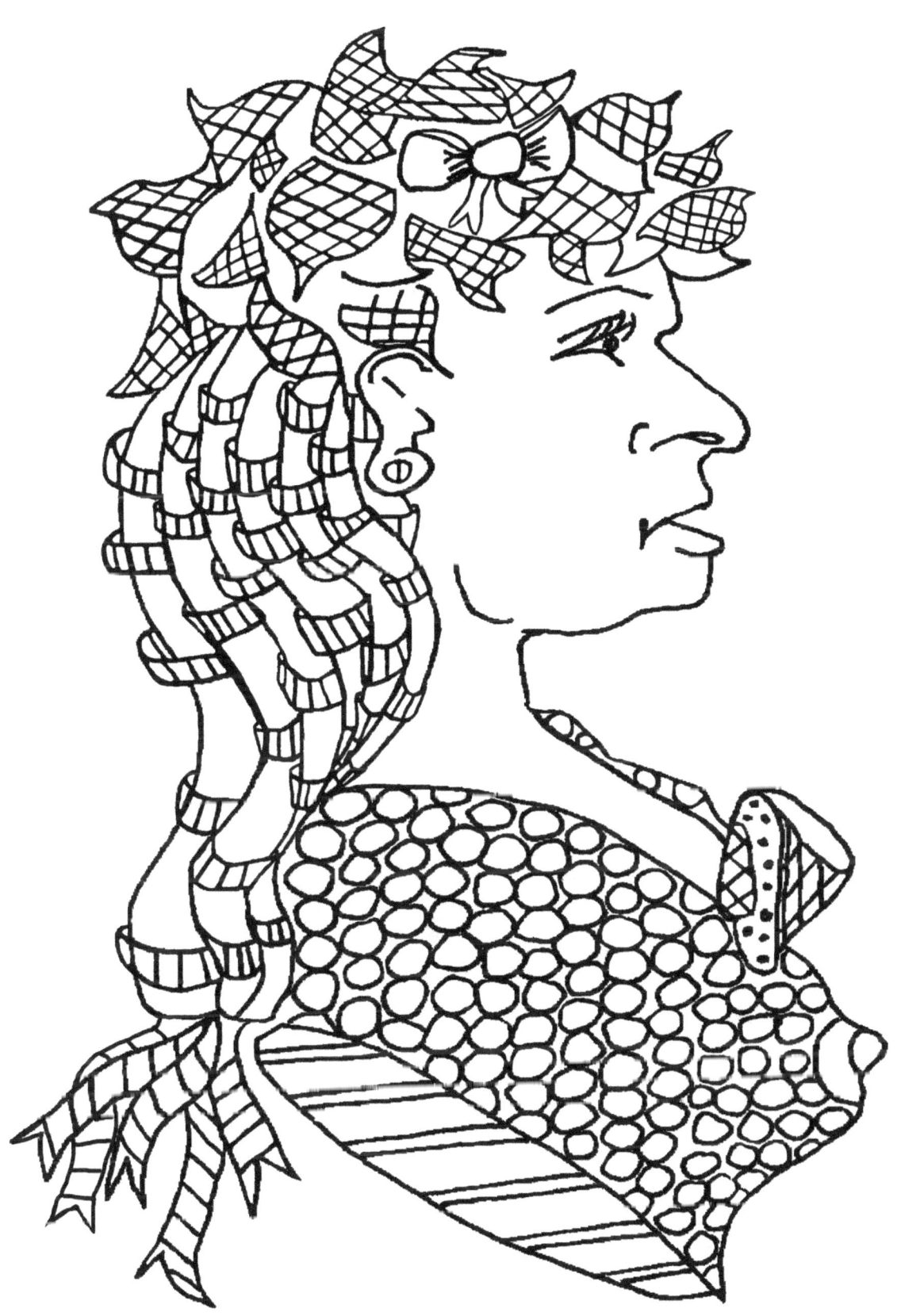

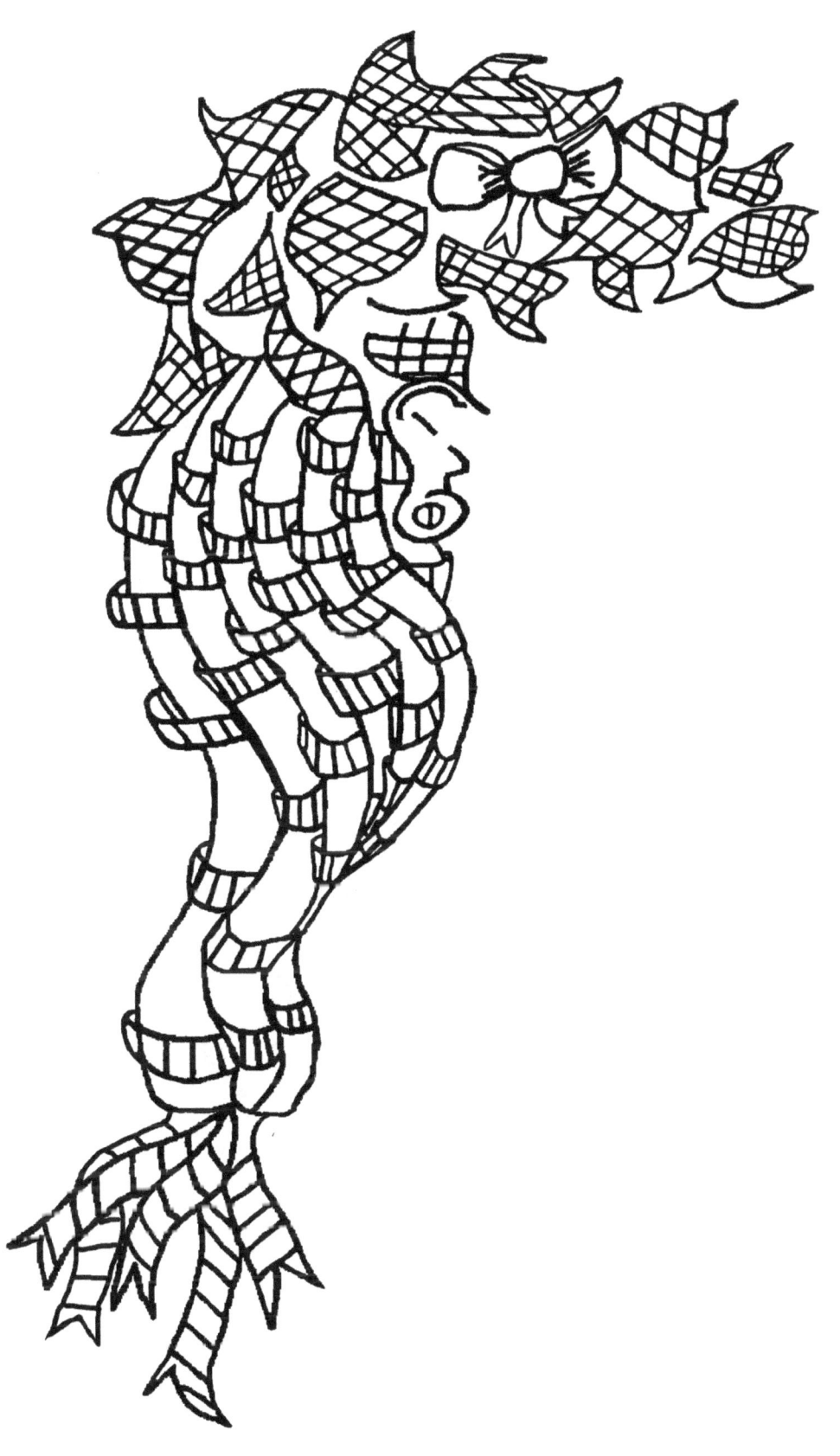

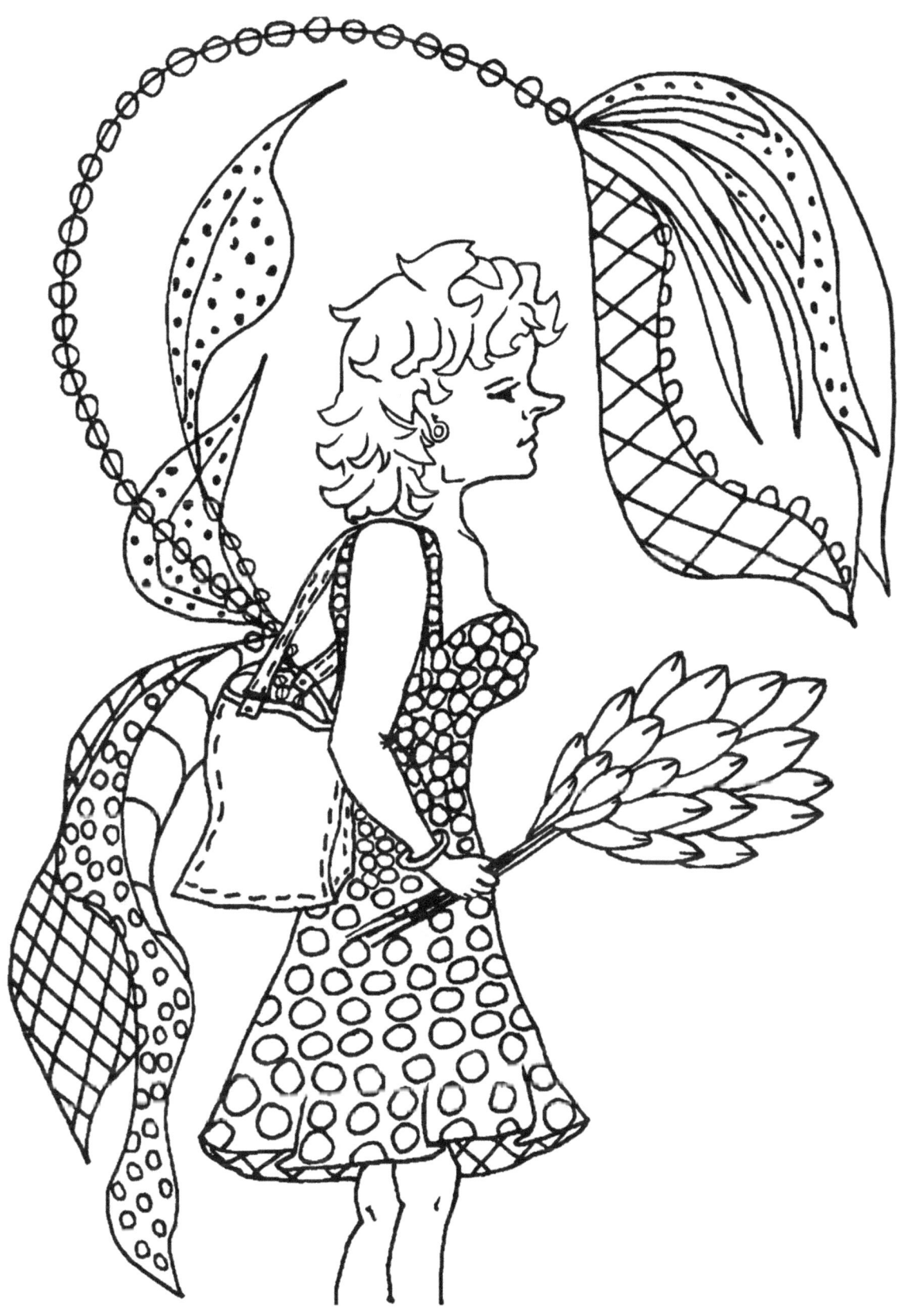

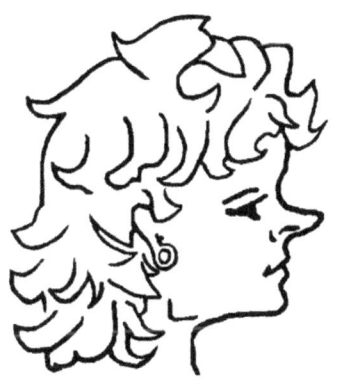

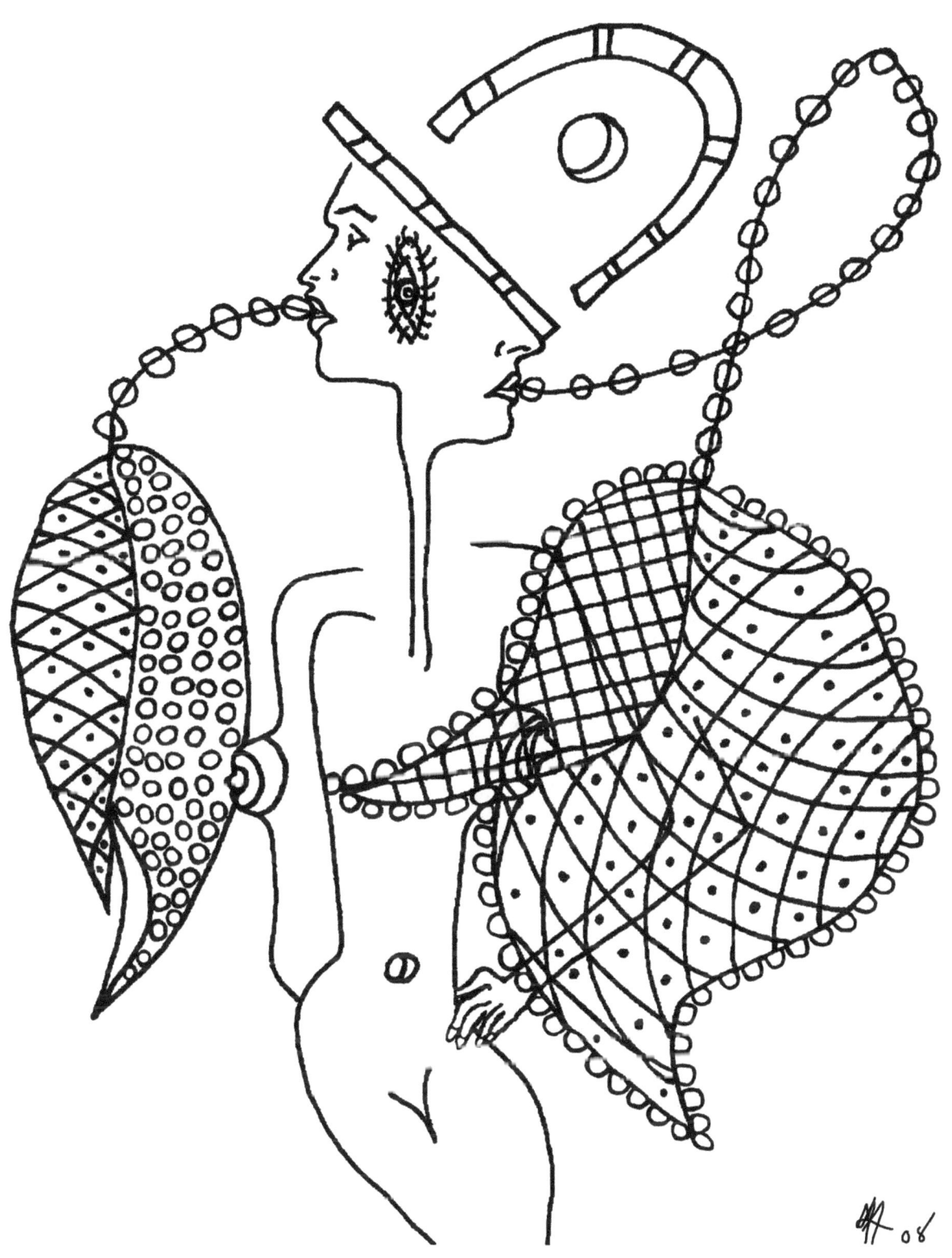

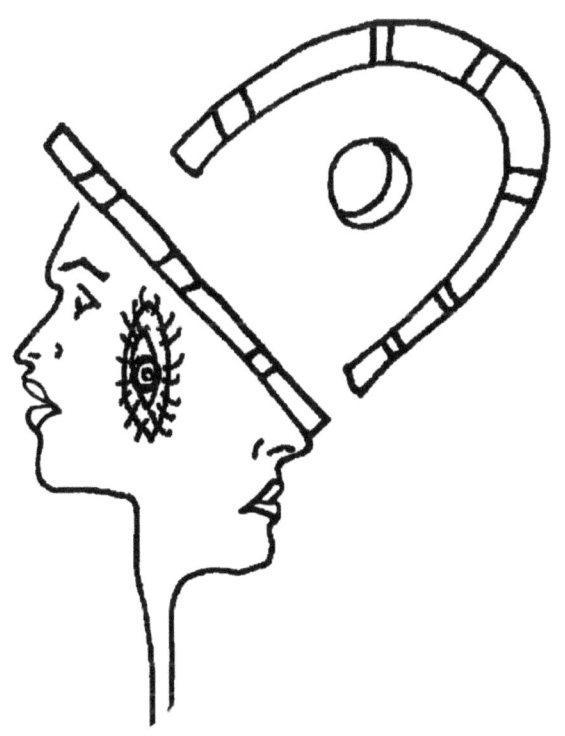

finish the drawing

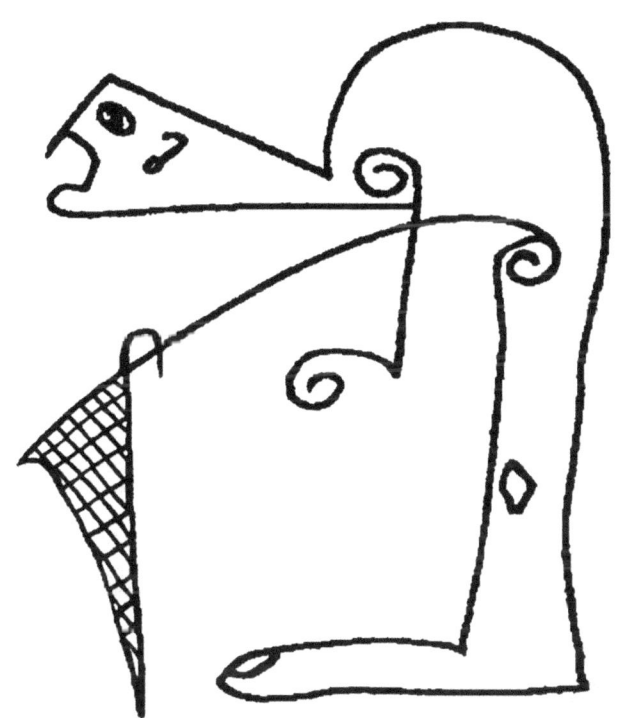

What's in a drawing?

Artists who have influenced my drawings the most are German artists Otto Dix (1891-1969) and George Grosz (1893-1959). Spanish artist Pablo Picasso (1881-1973) and British artist/illustrator Aubrey Beardsley (1872-1898). These artists, especially Otto Dix and George Grosz, who were very much influenced by World War Two, looked at the macabre and the sometimes seedier side of life around them.

Drawings are a very personal thing, catching a moment in time. We all have the ability to draw in our own way and can create our own style. In this book I have cropped some of my drawings for you to finish using your own imagination or real life studies. As you have more space on the page you can use vanishing points and perspective (objects that seem smaller as they go off into the distance, try this out using two same size oranges, put one orange close by and the other a few metres away, observe how small the orange looks furthest away).

If you are not used to drawing, use pencil first before going over the pencil lines with a black gel pen, when using pens put a cardboard under the page so that you do not spoil the drawing on the next page. When the gel ink is dry gently rub out the pencil lines. Using a gel pen gives more freedom and lets your drawing flow more easily when drawing from imagination. Set the mood and image you want to create in your minds eye and then begin.
Good luck.

Page for your own drawing

page for testing your colours

page for testing your colours